Where Is "Christ" in Christ-ians?

TOMEKA MARK

ISBN 978-1-64079-245-6 (Paperback)
ISBN 978-1-64079-246-3 (Digital)

Christian Faith Publishing, Inc.
296 Chestnut Street
Meadville, PA 16335
www.christianfaithpublishing.com

Printed in the United States of America

Contents

Dedication

My Heavenly Father: I dedicate this book to the One who saw me fit to undertake this project. I pray that it is everything You wanted it to be and that You will continue to guide me along this journey.

To Mom and Pop: My biggest fans. You encouraged and pushed me along the way. There were tough times, but you never let me give up. Your strength, courage, love, and prayer have helped me along this journey.

Acknowledgements

To God be the glory!

I first must thank my Lord and Savior who is the author and finisher of my faith. He saw something in me that I could not see in myself. I am so grateful. I would also like to thank my family members who are a part of our Tuesday night prayer who prayed and encouraged me along the way: my mom (Rose), Pop (Herbert), Larry, Lisa, Aunt Betty, Uncle Robert, Ezekiel, Noah, and Aunt Vivian, who is no longer with us. They are the original members, but we have expanded now, and I thank them as well. I would like to thank A&W services for all their support. I would like to thank my father Cleaster, brothers Larry and Raynard, and all my family and friends for their prayer and support.

Dear God,

I am forever grateful that You chose a nobody like me to do something for You. You saw something in me that I did not see in myself. I would not have thought in a million years that I would be chosen to help such a holy, righteous, and powerful God. I am scared and excited at the same time, but with Your help, I am going to do my very best to fulfill my purpose. I will seek direction from You before I make any decision. I will follow Your lead. It is not about me, but You, my Heavenly Father. So, please help me make this book become everything You envision, and help it go as far as You want. Please help it to touch and change the lives of those You choose it to reach.

God, while You are taking this book to the places it is supposed to go, prepare me to be a good representative. Impart in me the wisdom, knowledge, and understanding that I need to complete these tasks as well as any other that You have destined for me. God, I know some are going to ridicule and reject me. I know that comes with the calling, but that it is nothing compared to what You had to endure. Lord, help me to keep my head up because it is not about me. Please send some real saints to help me along my journey. Lord, go with me every step of the way, and protect me and my family from hurt, harm, and danger. God, I love you so much and want to please you in all ways. I am not perfect, but I am striving. Please forgive me when I fall short. Give me the strength, integrity, and power to overcome the trials and tribulations that lie ahead.

Thank you for choosing me!

Your humble servant,
Tomeka

"Christ" Checks

1. Are you a Christian?
2. If so, why?
3. What makes you different than any person who does not consider himself a Christian?
4. Do you believe in the theory of "once saved, always saved"? Why or why not?
5. How often do you read your Bible and pray?
6. Do you share the gospel with unbelievers?

Introduction

This book is a message from Christ. There are a lot of things that He sees that really sadden His heart. In this book, Christ is addressing six areas: church, schools, the workplace, saints, relationships, and Christmas, an occasion that honors his birth. Christ is calling us to evaluate ourselves. He wants us to check our motives to see if we are adapting Christian principles in our daily lives. In the eyes of God, we are living defeated worldly lives. We are barely praying, reading our Bibles, or sharing the gospel.

We, as His children, are putting Him in a box until Sunday. In the visible church, there are so many unfriendly members, so much pride and such a lack of love that people feel more love in the world than among the "church folks." We are allowing our schools to turn into places where sex, drugs, and violence are the norm. Children are not able to pray or learn about Christ. That being said, how can we be surprised of the outcome? Greed in the workplace has caused many to lose faith because they cannot see past their situations.

The loss of jobs or the stress of being overworked makes some turn to temporary, ungodly solutions. With all the hustle and bustle of our everyday lives, the saints are not being well represented. The lack of concern for others' needs and lack of willingness to really live for Christ do not draw anyone to Him. The high divorce rate among His children really hurts Him. How is it that we, His children, cannot establish stable relationships? Our relationships should be examples for the world to see. One of the most hurtful things He sees is being removed from celebrating Christmas, his birth.

This message is delivered in the first person, as Christ is speaking directly to us. This book can be used for Bible study, self-study, or group discussion. The book will give you questions after each chapter to check if you are applying Christian principles in your life. Even though we may read this and be sad or convicted, we know that our Father is a forgiving and loving God, waiting with open arms to receive us as we repent and get back on track.

"This people draweth nigh unto me with their mouth, and honoureth me with their lips; but their heart is far from me" (Matthew 15:8).

Chapter 1

Where Is "Christ" in the Church?

The purpose of the church is to teach sound doctrine to My children and deal lovingly and fairly with all the people in the church. The church is organized so I (Christ) can be glorified. The church is also a place of refuge. A church is where I come to meet my children, and they can praise and worship me. A church is a place to unchain yourself of all the things that have you bound. You come to be fed with your spiritual food. "Man shall not live by bread alone, but by every word that proceedeth out of the mouth of God" (Matthew 4:4). Of ultimate importance in the life of the church is to know Christ, work together in love and harmony, and spread the gospel to the world. But I do not see this in the churches. *Where am I?*

The word "church" is used in two senses: the invisible and the visible churches. The invisible church of God is not an organization on Earth consisting of people and buildings; it is really a supernatural entity comprised of those who are saved by Jesus. The visible churches, on the other hand, are buildings people attend for worship and to gain knowledge about our Savior, Jesus Christ. The visible church is divided into different religious organizations or beliefs. Individuals attend the church of their preference, but the common goal is to prepare the people for the coming of the Lord. The visible churches are Bible-based teaching churches. I am very disappointed that the churches are not teaching the whole truth.

The leaders of the churches are watering down my word to please the people and teaching popular sermons to make people feel good. The biggest concern for most churches is filling up the pews with their large congregations. I will hold you accountable for your disobedience. I would be very pleased if all the visible churches and religious assemblies would come together and teach the gospel. The focus should not be about whose religious beliefs are right and whose are wrong. The focus should be to win souls for the kingdom.

You should know that I am the way "the truth and the light, no one comes before my father but through me" (John 14:6). Your focus should be to know me and allow me to direct your path. One of My biggest disappointments in the church is not speaking up and calling *sin* what it is—"sin," "a deliberate act against the law of God" (1 John 3:4). Leaders in the visible churches are not speaking up against sin because they do not want to be harsh on the people. They are responsible for teaching as well as being a living example. This is where there is a gap. They cannot teach what they do not live. The lack of teaching on holiness in the visible churches is not an excuse for My children to *sin*. You are responsible for reading and knowing the Word for yourself. You cannot put the responsibility of your soul in someone else's hands. "Wherefore, my beloved, as ye have always obeyed, not as in my presence only, but now much more in my absence, work out your own salvation with fear and trembling" (Philippians 2:12).

I (Christ) know there is a lot of confusion with all the different religions and various beliefs.

You are longing for something that you cannot get from a man, a religion, or a building—a connection, a touch from me that can change your whole life. The leaders in the visible churches need stop the same Sunday-after-Sunday routine and allow My glory to fill the house. This will allow My children to experience signs, wonders, and miracles.

Signs, Wonders, and Miracles

Signs and *wonders* refer to the miracles produced by the Holy Spirit, such as through the apostles, especially Paul, as a testimony to God's power and glory. We can see these portrayed in many places in Scripture (Exodus 7:3; Deuteronomy 4:3, 6:22, and 7:19; Isaiah 8:18; Daniel 6:27; and book of Acts). Also referred to as *powers* and *miracles,* these are instruments that point to God's confirmation, as He used supernatural activities that are beyond our limited knowledge and comprehension to prove His point and demonstrate His Word. They were also used to show the authority of the apostles and those sent by God, such as Stephen who healed people who were sick beyond current medical knowledge. This was the authentic witness and proof of God. Signs are never pointed to themselves or the human performer; rather, they point to the person and work of Christ (Acts 2:4-12, 22, 43; 3:7-9, 11-12, 16; 4:30; 6:8; 14:3; and 15:12; Romans 15:19; 2 Corinthians 12:4-12; and Hebrews 2:4; 6:1-12).

This is the supernatural power that I have but barely able to let loose to do things for My children. I am kept in a box. The lack of faith and holy living keeps My children away from experiencing the real deliverance and breakthroughs that is so needed.

Five-Fold Ministry

I (Christ) know the reason why there is a routine service in most visible churches. Leaders are running a one-man ministry. They have jobs, families, and ministries. That takes away their time for seeking and preparing fresh Word. In some cases, there are people who can assist when needed. But most of the time, the pastor plays multiple roles, and this causes stress. This is the reason why many pastors are struggling with depression and suicidal thoughts and ministries are closing. I established the five-fold ministry for the building of my kingdom not just a pastor, as it is in most churches today. "It was he who gave some to be apostles, some to be prophets, some to be evangelists, and some to be pastors and teachers, to prepare God's people for works of service, so that the body of Christ may be built up until we all reach unity in the faith and in the knowledge of the Son of God and become mature, attaining to the whole measure of the fullness of Christ" (Ephesians 4:11-13).

The different religious beliefs established by men is causing many gifts to be restricted. The many denominations have their roles. They are comfortable with their reverends, deacons, elders, etc. When an apostle or prophet enters and starts to use their gifts, they get insecure and afraid of what will be exposed. The leaders stop them from ministering. The five-fold has various gifts that are needed for the body.

I want the body to use discernment when working with the different roles and gifts. They each have uniqueness that will add value to building the kingdom. I designed it according to what I know is needed to bring in the flock and build them up to go out. My leaders, please know the roles. I am giving you a description that can help determine if anyone is out of their role.

These gifts are given for three purposes:

1. To perfect the saints (perfecting—complete furnishing; equipping)
2. For the work of the ministry (ministry—service; ministering)
3. To edify the body of Christ (edifying—build up; promote growth)

It just so happens that these are the reasons these gifts are given, but there is also a process that is given. The gifts are not only doing these three things but also helping the saints carry out these three things. I need leaders to fully understand the gifts and to understand the meaning of the names given to each one.

- Apostle—one who is sent
- Prophet—interpreter of oracles that are hidden
- Evangelist—bringer of good tidings

- Pastors—shepherd; herdsman
- Teachers—one fit to teach; master; doctor

Below is a definition to each gift in a descriptive way of function.

Evangelist—An evangelist is someone who is sent to save souls and present the gospel message. We see evangelists where the lost are, and they are not listed in the order of the church in 1 Corinthians 12:28. Marks of an evangelist are salvations and healings and miracles. They have the ability to touch hardened hearts with God's love for them to receive salvation. They also are found in the midst of environments that breed sin. The word is only used three times in Scripture. The best example of an evangelist is Stephen. Philip started his ministry as a deacon in the helps ministry, in Acts 6:1, and moved into calling, in Acts 8:26-40. They are generally drawn to pastors. They are trans-local who, as a rule, travel by themselves.

The characteristics of an evangelist are the following:

- Displays supernatural advertising of signs and wonders, words of knowledge
- Preaches the gospel of Jesus only
- Preaches the Word, not the church doctrine
- Has an ability to bring people to an individual decision
- Frees the people
- Does not have responsibility inside church walls
- Active—always in motion
- Aggressive and bold—do bold and crazy things
- Transient—move around
- Called to the world not the church—called outside of the church walls
- Has an anointing for the lost and finding opening to hearts
- Burns for lost souls and wins them to Christ—the most driving force in them
- Intolerant to church's laziness for outreaches and witnessing
- Has great faith and trusts God for money because churches do not support them

- Longs for mass salvations
- Preaches simple message of salvation
- Doesn't care about opposition confronting the enemy head on
- Leaves people joyful and rejoicing after speaking

Pastor—The word pastor is only used one time in Scripture, yet we have made it the primary function today. Pastors are nurturers and must lay their lives down for the flock. They are healers of the broken and are given oversight to make sure the needs of the people are being met. Just like a herdsman, there are also undershepherds or pastors in almost every body of believers. They may not be recognized but are active, meeting the needs of and ministering healing to others. Pastors are drawn to teachers to evangelist and then to teachers. Pastors are most effective in one on ones and modeling Christ. Not all pastors will be dynamic teachers, but they will be dynamic in showing love. They were never placed as final oversight or vision casters to the people. They are always given to a set group of people.

Description of office of pastors are as follows:

- Pastors have a love for the people.
- They must have compassion for the people and the church.
- They have a giving attitude instead of taking.
- Pastors return love for hate when criticized.
- They look for the ones who are hurting and focus on them until healed or whole.
- They never give up on people because they have a huge heart
- They see the good, finished, and complete person.
- They have a special grace for the office.
- They have a gift for teaching and the ability to share life experiences in counseling.
- They are overprotective of their sheep.
- They have long patience.
- They believe that shepherds should be among the sheep.

- They are settled, and they remain for the long haul.
- They need wisdom, knowledge, and discerning of spirits, not for leading a body but for ministering the hurts of the people.

Teacher—The office of the teacher is one that stirs others to know the truth. It is more than explaining; it carries an anointing that brings change. Teachers love the truth, and they love to study. They are avid readers and study topics in multiple ways. They are generally scribes and historians. They expand on what the apostles release and prophets speak, so others can clearly understand. They teach line upon line. They carry a divine, supernatural ability to impart knowledge beyond the natural way of doing. True teachers will never teach doctrinal error but will study in-depth before giving a new insight. They are an office with a main thrust to study and give away what they have learned. Teachers explain things from many different angles, so the person is sure to understand.

Teachers are willing to be taught. They can be local and trans-local in ministry assignments as they are given to the body as a whole. They generally travel by themselves and sometimes with apostles and prophets.

Teachers function to do the following:

- Inspire—light a fire
- Lay a foundation and then build upon that foundation
- Build upon other ministries
- Always build up
- Teach you into correction without you knowing it
- Counsel—teachers will hand you a tape or book
- Convey the Word of God in-depth
- Become teachable
- Have a love for books
- Hunger and thirst for knowledge and truth
- Get a revelation from a prophet then teach on it
- Become very organized people

- Have a love for the Word of God
- Leave you desiring for more
- Transfer the truth
- Teachers who are pastors of a church, repeat in three to five year cycles

Prophet—Prophets speak from the revelation of the heart of God in a matter. It is not by perception, but by inspiration. They are foretellers and revealers of the intentions of God. They move in the inspirational gifts of 1 Corinthians 12 through words of wisdom, prophecy, and knowledge. *It is not by perception, but by inspiration.*

This office requires a consistent manifestation of at least two of the revelation gifts on an ongoing basis.

Most prophets also experience prophetic dreams filled with symbolism and visions. Prophets speak more than just individual prophetic words. They speak prophetic words or messages that shift spiritual atmospheres over regions. They generally are drawn to the apostles. The number one job of prophets is not to prophesy but to train the people to hear God. When people can hear God in a region, it is just as great or even greater than a prophet releasing word over a region! They are generally trans-local as they are given to the body as a whole. They travel by themselves and with apostles.

Attributes of the office of a prophet are as follows:

- Many think all a prophet does is prophesy.
- A prophet needs to be a preacher or teacher of the Word
- Laying on of hands goes with it.
- Generally healing goes with it (Luke 4:27).
- Generally, the miraculous goes with it (II Kings 5:33).
- Many people think prophets should know everything.
- Many people think that any time they want, a prophet can give a word; they only do as the Spirit wills.
- Prophets are only human.
- Prophets hearts are broken over sin.
- Prophets speak words in season.

- New Testament prophets speak words of correction sandwiched in love.
- Prophets speak directional confirming words.
- A prophet of God is a messenger of God's will—not doctrine.
- A prophet initiated no messages or sermons from his own will *in the name of the Lord.*
- A prophet speaks only new revealed words from God.
- A prophet has to be commanded by God to speak.
- A prophet is not allowed to speak any error in God's name.
- A prophet's prediction of the Old Testament has to come true or he would be branded a false prophet and be executed, thus limiting his ability to learn from his mistakes and to again mislead the people of God.
- Prophecy is the very voice of Christ speaking to the church!

Apostle—With so much confusion and lack of understanding, we will spend a little more time on this gifting. It is a governmental gift given to bring the church into order and increased authority and anointing. Most apostles are intolerant of doctrinal error as it makes their jobs harder. There have always been apostles; we have just not recognized them. The humility they operate in will promote themselves as such. Apostles are forerunners, and they introduce new dimensions of spirit life. They are focused on kingdom over an individual body. They are transient and are given to the body. All apostles are fathers, but not all fathers are apostles. They see the gifts in people and have an ability to bring those gifting out. Since they have been called to perfect the saints, they see all truth and not just one aspect of truth. While pastoral truth deals with the individual life, apostolic truth deals with overall effect on the body. Pastoral truth produces self-serving servants; apostolic truths produce body-serving sons. Apostle is the only office Jesus appointed, and the only office commissioned in Scripture.

An apostle is sent with a message and a specific assignment and mandate given by God directly for a specific people, cause, and purpose directly concerning the Kingdom of God. This message releases people from the past, confronts the present, and establishes the future. The fruit of apostleship is evident by their love for correct doctrine and intolerance of false concepts and teaching. They are writers of books and establishers of schools and training and have put in place dynamics that continue to expand and grow when they are no longer around. Birthing a church does not make a person an apostle; an evangelist can do this. Running a large church does not make a person an apostle; a good administrator can do this. All apostles have lived a life of suffering for righteousness' sake to establish the kingdom. All apostles have seen the Lord, and this defined their personal lives and molded their sprits.

All apostles have a cross section of voluntary followers, more than a local congregation, who have benefitted from the apostles and have functional relationship with them. Apostles are counselors to other ministries and investors into emerging ministries. These gifts are attracted to apostles because they know the apostle will know how to place them and how to make them grow into the gift they are to be. The main thing to realize is that apostles are given to bring order, establish churches or ministries, and bring out the other ministry gifts. They carry resurrection life and apostolic grace that set them apart. They are given to the whole body of Christ and so are trans-local. They travel by themselves and with prophets. Every apostle has something of significance they are Apostilling.

An apostle's functions include the following:

1. Has been commissioned, ordained, and sent with purpose and mission
2. Pioneers and takes risks
3. Carries the spirit of resurrection and reformation—brings life and spiritual flow
4. Depends on God's approval and not mans
5. Sets things in order and maintains spiritual flow
6. Ministers out of their experience and not out of their head—pulls people out of their comfort zone

7. Is ahead of their time—visionaries
8. Attracts other ministry gifts
9. Produces like-minded sons and daughters of the same faith
10. Draws other gifts to them, trains them, and then releases them into ministry
11. Has unique spiritual authority in the body of Christ and over territories
12. Has a specific assignment. One of the most distinguishing marks of an apostle is the ability to embrace all other ministry gifts.

Attributes of an apostle are the following:

- Teacher and preacher of the Word
- Has spiritual gifts—flow in all gifts
- Has deep personal experience
- Has an ability to establish churches or ministries
- Has spiritual leadership
- Is sent by the Holy Ghost
- Is a father figure—spiritually mature
- Has broad oversight—vision of body as a whole
- Walks in spiritual authority
- Called to a region or a people
- Has the ability to draw other gifts to them
- Has a heart for the people
- Is a spiritual covering—cover other gifts
- Has patience
- Followed by signs and wonders
- Does mighty deeds
- Has vision for the church
- Labors night and day
- Looks upon self as father and congregation as children
- Taught by God
- Minister in the power of God, not the wisdom of men
- Manifests the living God

- Leads by Christ's example
- Pleases God, not men
- Does not flatter men
- Is gentle with the saints
- Is holy, righteous, and blameless
- Exhorts, comforts, and chastens as necessary
- Takes glory in the glorious church
- Endures hardship and persecution for the church's sake

I (Christ) have given you a good understanding of the roles in the five-fold ministry. I ask that you, as leaders, establish this structure in your church or ministry. This is what is needed in the body to help build my kingdom effectively. The enemy has set churches up to fail by making leaders think they can build without having the five-fold structure. The prideful ego give leaders the minds that they can operate alone. Yes, I have given my children the ability to have gifts in multiple areas. No one person can do all the role efficiently, as you will be pulled into many areas or roles. This leaves leaders tired and ineffective. The results are a sick, unhealthy spiritual body.

This is what the enemy wants to see; my children in bondage—defeated and disconnected. When my leaders are stretched and overworked, the enemy uses that to try to cause chaos in the lives of their sheep, taking them on an up-and-down ride where they do not know who I am. They do not know who they are in me. The power that is available to them through my Spirit. They settle for living a meaningless life constantly falling into *sin*.

Spiritual Warfare

This is why I (Christ) ask that my children be prepared for spiritual warfare at all times. What is a spiritual warfare? Spiritual warfare is the Christian concept of taking a stand against preternatural evil forces. It is based on the belief in evil spirits that are able to intervene in human affairs. It is an invisible war with demons, Satan, and the power of darkness. Most of my children are living as if there is no invisible war.

Spiritual warfare is an epic battle between good and evil which began when Satan was cast out of heaven. This confrontation escalated to the Garden of Eden, where the first man, Adam, received a near-fatal blow that echoed throughout the history of God's people. I (Christ) came to the Earth and faced this battle daily. The devil tempted me in the wilderness, and the battle raged. I was sent to the cross to die... and the battle raged. I rose victoriously on the third day... but the enemy still hasn't surrendered. "For we do not wrestle against flesh and blood, but against principalities, against powers, against the rulers of the darkness of this age, against spiritual *hosts* of wickedness in the heavenly *places*" (Ephesians 6:12).

Surrounding us is a spiritual war—angels vs. demon, good vs. evil, and light vs. darkness. But amazingly, most believers live as if this conflict is not even happening, as if the "battle of the ages" is just a fantasy or sci-fi story. Yet, not one of us is immune to the consequences of spiritual warfare. Although the players fight in an invisible realm, we all face the effects—pain, struggle, defeat, and heartache—of their conflict every day of our lives.

Until you recognize that your struggle is not with man but with spiritual hosts of wickedness in the heavenly places, you will never begin to live in victory. Your victory in spiritual warfare must rest on the reality that I (Christ) have given you everything that you need to live in the light of the truth of His victory, in order to experience and become all that I have created you to be. But I will not dress you in the weapons of warfare.

You are going to have to put on the Armor of God yourself—everyday—in order to experience the victory that is yours. "Finally, my brethren, be strong in the Lord and in the power of His might. *Put on the whole armor of God, that you may be able to stand against the wiles of the devil*" (Ephesians 6:10-18).

My battle plan over spiritual warfare: "And ye shall tread down the wicked; for they shall be ashes under the soles of your feet in the day that I shall do this, saith the Lord of hosts" (Malachi 4:3).

I. *Every child of God has been given a promise of victory over Satan.*

Isaiah 54:17 "No weapon that is formed against thee shall prosper; and every tongue that shall rise against thee in judgment thou shalt condemn. This is the heritage of the servants of the Lord..."

Malachi 4:3 "And you shall tread down the wicked; for they shall be ashes under the soles of your feet in the day that I shall do this, saith the Lord of hosts."

Luke 10:19 "Behold, I give unto you power to tread on serpents and scorpions, and over all the power of the enemy: and nothing shall by any means hurt you."

Romans 8:38-39 "For I am persuaded that neither death, nor life, nor angels, nor principalities, nor powers...nor height, nor depth, nor any other creature, shall be able to separate us from the love of God, which is in Christ Jesus our Lord."

James 4:7 "...Resist the devil, and he will flee from you."

1 John 4:4 "You...have overcome them: because greater is He that is in you, than he that is in the world."

II. *It is important that we recognize who our enemy is and what his tactics are.*

"For we are not ignorant of his (Satan's) devices." (2 Corinthians 2:11)

A. Our battle is "not against flesh and blood" (things in the natural realm), "but against...spiritual wickedness." "For though we walk in the flesh, we do not war after the flesh. For the weapons of our warfare are not carnal…" (2 Corinthians 10:3-5; Ephesians 6:12)

B. Authority must be taken over Satan's attempts to hinder the work and the Word of God. There are spiritual powers that must be broken (Daniel 10:12-13;1 Thessalonians 2:18).

C. Satan's main device is deception.

    1. Subtlety.
Genesis 3:1 "Now the serpent was more subtle than any beast of the field…"; 2 Corinthians 11:3

    2. Doubt.
Genesis 3:1 "Yea, hath God said…?"
Luke 4:3, 9; Matthew 4:3, 6 "If thou be the Son of God…if…"

    3. Lies.
Genesis 3:4; John 8:44

III. *The Bible uses several metaphors to describe the "fight of faith" (1 Timothy 6:12) that the believer must wage against the evil one.*

A. Boxer.
1 Corinthians 9:26 "I therefore so run, not as uncertainly; so fight I, not as one that beateth the air…"

B. Soldier.
2 Timothy 2:3-5 "Thou therefore endure hardness, as a good soldier of Jesus Christ. No man that warreth entangleth himself with the affairs of this life; that he may please him who hath chosen him to be a soldier."

Ephesians 6:11-17 "Put on the whole Armor of God, that ye may be able to stand against the wiles of the devil… take unto you the whole Armor of God, that ye may be able to withstand in the evil day, and having done all, to stand. Stand therefore…"

C. Wrestler.
Ephesians 6:12 "For we wrestle not against flesh and blood, but against principalities, against powers, against the rulers of the darkness of this world, against spiritual wickedness in high places."

IV. *What does it mean to "resist the devil?" How can this be done?*

A. The Armor of God.
Ephesians chapter 6

1. Truth (v. 14)
2. Righteousness (v. 14)
3. Salvation (v. 17; 1 Thessalonians 5:8)
4. The gospel of peace (v. 15)
5. Faith (v. 14; 1 Thessalonians 5:8)

Paul says that faith is of primary importance: "above all…"

Ephesians 6:16 "Above all, taking the shield of faith, wherewith ye shall be able to quench all the fiery darts of the wicked."

1 Peter 5:8-9 "Be sober, be vigilant; because your adversary the devil, as a roaring lion, walketh about, seeking whom he may devour: whom resist steadfast in the faith…"

1 John 5:4-5 "For whatsoever is born of God overcometh the world: and this is the victory that overcometh the world, even our faith…"

B. But faith and the word are inseparable.
1. The word did not profit them, not being mixed with faith (Hebrews 4:2).

2. Yet faith comes through the word ("rhema") of God (Romans 10:17).

3. It must be both by confession of the mouth and belief in the heart (Romans 10:9).

6. The Word of God (Ephesians 6:17; Mark 11:24-25; Numbers 13:30)

    A. It was the spoken ("rhema") word that Jesus used in confronting the devil in the wilderness. He did not recite miscellaneous scriptures to the devil, but delivered the word of God with authority and power (Luke 4:4, 10, 12).

    B. Notice that this is the only offensive part of the armor, referred to in scripture as a "two-edged sword" (Psalms 149:6-9; Ephesians 6:17; Hebrews 4:12; Revelation 2:16).

    C. The weapon of praise (Numbers 10:9, 35; 31:6-7; 1 Samuel 16:23; 2 Chronicles 20:21-22 (Note especially the fact that it was their initiative: "when they began..."); Psalms 68:1-2; 149:5-9; Isaiah 33:3; Joel 2; Acts 16:24-26).

    D. The anointing (1 Samuel 16:14-23; Isaiah 10:27).

    E. Prayer (Luke 22:31-32).

V. *To stand victoriously in battle against the enemy, certain spiritual requirements must be met in the life of the believer.*

    A. Obedience (Deuteronomy 11:22-25; Deuteronomy 28:1, 7)

    B. A right relationship with God (Deuteronomy 11:22-25; Psalm 91)

    C. No area of the life left exposed to the devil: giving him no foothold (Ephesians 4:27)

VI. *It is the responsibility of the believer to prepare for battle, to put on the whole Armor of God" (Ephesians 6:11), and to "stand against the evil one" (vv. 11-14)—these are active verbs. But it is God who fights the battle. Indeed, Jesus Christ has already defeated the enemy for us. We must simply walk in the victory (Deuteronomy 20:1; 2 Chronicles 20:15; Colossians 2:15)!*

Many churches will not be prepared to come back with me. I will be looking for a sinless church, *"that he might present it to himself a glorious church, not having spot, or wrinkle, or any such thing; but that it should be holy and without blemish"* (Ephesians 5:27). Churches, I am holding you accountable for not teaching the people about salvation. Salvation is glorification—God's future reward for His obedient children. It is by grace you have been saved through faith, and *this is not your own doing;* it is the gift of God—not the result of works, so that no one may boast (Ephesians 2:8-9).

For a sinner to be saved, he must first hear the gospel preached (Romans 10:17). Then, the Spirit must convict him of sin so that he can repent, be baptized in the name of Jesus Christ for the remission of sins, and receive the gift of the Holy Ghost (Acts 2:38). Finally, the newly converted person (no longer a sinner) must be led by the Spirit throughout his life (Romans 8:14). This is how sinners are saved, and this is what I came to do. Another issue that I have with my churches is the prosperity teachings. This is a popular message running through the churches.

The congregations are filled with capacity because the man of God is about to teach them how to be rich by applying my word. The principle of living your life according to my word is not being taught. Everybody thinks if I "sow" God will "grow." But the problem is that the leaders are the only ones prospering. Church leaders have made prosperity filthy in my eyes. People are looking to church leaders as role models because many of them are rich and famous. Some leaders are using my desperate and hurting children to help furnish their lavish lifestyles. They have taken ministry to another level; they request their own personal transportation (planes, limousines, etc.) and refuse to take public means of transportation or even drive for themselves.

I said, *"I walked the streets and rode donkeys wherever I needed to go to do my Father's will"* (Matthew 5:21). Are you performing miracles? Are you doing the works I did? I did all these things for the glory of God, not for a monetary price. You are only going to the places that can give you the right price. You are charging my children to give them the Word that you are getting from me for free. I paid the price for their salvation. Remember, you are just a servant who I am speaking through to get a message out to my children. Now, you are attaching a big price to yourself before delivering the message. While you are preaching, I come to my children when they cry out to me, praise me, or worship me. Leaders, you are not bringing me in your pockets and letting me free to do my work.

The way things are being presented, it is as though you are the mediator between my children and me, as if my children cannot be healed unless you have a healing service. I heal, deliver, and destroy yokes, for free. Now you, on the other hand, cannot do anything without me, but you charge a big price just to show up. Are you saying your presence is much more valuable than mine? I have children who are starving and homeless, and you choose to keep up with your lavish lifestyle when you see all of this around you. Where am I? Leaders, check your motives before you get behind the pulpit to preach a sermon. Is this for the building of my kingdom or yours? Once again, I am asking, *Where am I?*

Among all the other problems that I see in the churches, you allow anyone to be church leaders, which is not acceptable. There are homosexuals in high positions in the church even though my word is against molestation, homosexuality, and any uncleanness (Leviticus. 18:22; 20:13, 12:15). Homosexuality is one of the deepest issues dividing the churches today. The devil is using this spirit to trick so many of my children. You are allowing this spirit to involve you in unnatural behavior.

You are taking something I created to be shared by a husband and wife and making it filthy. The most horrible part is that the church is taking my word and trying to justify this behavior. Yes, I (Christ) said, *"Thou shalt love thy neighbor as thyself"* (Matthew 19:19b). You can still love the person but hate the sin or spirit that is controlling their life. *For we wrestle not against flesh and blood, but against principalities, against powers, against the rulers of the darkness of this world, against spiritual wickedness in high places* (Ephesians 6:12).

Come together as a body of Christ and be of one accord when fighting this spirit. You have to stand firm and take action against the spirits that are spreading as rapidly as this one. Homosexuality is in the churches and schools and has established its own community. This spirit is trying to establish its own lifestyle and is marketing it to make it seem normal.

The spirit of homosexuality is strong. It is trying to establish another version of the marriage and the family structure that I created. Now my children, you should know this spirit is not of Christ when it goes against my word. Stop allowing this spirit to establish an identity. It is not an alternative lifestyle.

There is no choice. You choose life or death. Study my word and know my ways. Do not water it down to nurture these spirits that are destroying so many lives and homes. Please stop believing that people are born homosexual. This is a lie from the pit of hell. I do not create anything that is an abomination to my word. Where am I? How can you allow these people to hold positions as bishops and allow them to teach my people? My leaders are supposed to be examples. I have qualifications in my word detailing what I want in my leaders (Titus 1:5-9). What type of example are they setting? Would you want your child to follow his path? That is not acceptable behavior.

It goes against my word and you should not allow this. The church is supposed to teach the truth. They are to teach things that will help my children be "saved" and stay "saved." The church was created to build the kingdom of God. It is not just a place where the saints go for fellowship. For sinners to go to church once a week and repent and then go back into the world to continue building the devil's kingdom that is unacceptable. The world is not coming out of darkness because the church is not showing them any reason. The church looks and acts just like the world. They are not operating in unity. *"Behold, how good and how pleasant it is for brethren to dwell together in unity"* (Psalms 133:1)! Religious beliefs have caused great separation within the church. There are congregations that worship a man as their form of Christ. They go to him and confess their sins for him to pardon.

I went through the pain on Calvary to carry the sins and burdens for all of my children. Now, you are confessing your sins to men and depending on someone to teach you everything about me. You are not reading my word or seeking me in prayer for yourselves. God is a jealous God. *"For thou shalt worship no other god: for the Lord, whose name is Jealous, is a jealous God"* (Exodus 34:14). *"I am the way, the truth and light. No one can get to the father but through me"* (John 14:6). You are hiding and covering up sin to keep people's reputation. You are concerned with keeping the churches filled and keeping the money to build big buildings. This religion has the biggest buildings and millions of people as followers. You need to repent and get in order. You will be held accountable for every lost soul that follows you. My wrath will come upon those who know right and choose to be disobedient. The church is supposed to teach about the choice between holiness and hell and not about denying the need of having my spirit in you to be "saved." I said: *Having a form of godliness, but denying the power thereof: from such turn away. For of this sort are they which creep into houses, and lead captive silly women laden with sins, led away with divers lusts, ever learning, and never able to come to the knowledge of the truth* (2 Timothy 3:5-7).

I also said, *"Except a man be born of water and of the Spirit, he cannot enter into the kingdom of God"* (John 3:5). Why do you pick and choose what you want to believe and then teach my children only part of the truth? *"Preach the Word. Be prepared in season and out of season; correct, rebuke and encourage with great patience and careful instruction"* (2 Timothy 4:2). You are not teaching them sound doctrine. I left people here to help perfect the saints. *"And he gave some, apostles; and some, prophets; and some, evangelists; and some, pastors and teachers; For the perfecting of the saints, for the work of the ministry, for the edifying of the body of Christ: Till we all come in the unity of the faith, and of the knowledge of the Son of God, unto a perfect man, unto the measure of the stature of the fulness of Christ"* (Ephesians 4:11-13). They are to prepare you to go out into the world and reach other lost souls for the kingdom. Man has made church a place where he competes against others leader for members, fancy buildings, and statuses.

He uses my house as a playground for his filthy and unclean behavior. Man has become so prideful and has no respect for my house or any fear of doing wrong. The church is also a place of worship and not a place for confusion, strife, and gambling. These types of things should not be happening in my house. The church is not keeping my house clean and respecting my word. Church leaders allow anyone to sing in the choir, preach, and be an active part of auxiliaries in the church without any accountability. The members drink, party, and do unclean things (fornicate, commit adultery, etc.) and still come to church Sunday after Sunday without feeling any conviction. Deliverance is needed, and you can only be set free by the Holy Ghost which gives you power from on high. *"I am going to send you what my Father has promised; but stay in the city until you have been clothed with power from on high"* (Luke 24:49).

My children should not keep living in sin. Churches, teach your members about repentance and turning away from their sinful ways. Teach them to fear me and keep my commandments. Some beliefs are concerned with tradition—being more concerned with the way a person dresses and your overall appearance. Instead, churches should just teach the gospel and salvation for their souls. People spend much time trying to look "holy," but their lifestyles are far from being holy. Churches are rejecting my name and my spirit. You have allowed a worldly spirit to come in and feel comfortable in the church. Sinners leave the service feeling good instead of feeling convicted, and this allows them to continue to live in sin, thinking I will forgive them and saying "God knows my heart." Yes, I do know everybody's heart. *"The heart is deceitful above all things, and desperately wicked: who can know it? I the Lord search the heart, I try the reins, even to give every man according to his ways, and according to the fruit of his doings"* (Jeremiah 17:9-10).

When will my visible churches come together and take a stand against all *sin*? When this happens, we will see that many will turn away from their sinful ways, and they will come to me. But with so much division among the churches, my children are confused as to where to worship. I say, *"One Lord, one faith, one baptism, One God and Father of all, who is above all, and through all, and in you all"* (Ephesians 4:5-6). The true church is the unseen or the invisible church. It is unseen except by Him who "searches the heart." *"The Lord knoweth them that are his"* (2 Timothy 2:19). The church, to which the attributes, prerogatives, and promises pertaining to Christ's kingdom belong, is a spiritual body consisting of all true believers: the invisible church. It's unity. It will continue through all ages until the end of the world. It can never be destroyed. It is an "everlasting kingdom."

Scriptures Against Homosexuality

Genesis 19:3-5, 10-11
But he (Lot) urged them {two angels appearing as men) strongly; so they turned aside to him and entered his house; and he made them a feast, and baked unleavened bread, and they ate. But before they lay down, the men of Sodom, both young and old, all the people to the last man, surrounded the house; and they called to Lot, "Where are the men who came to you tonight? Bring them out to us that we may know them." ...But the men (angels) put forth their hands and brought Lot into the house to them, and shut the door. And they struck with blindness the men who were at the door of the house.

Judges 19:22-23, 25
As they were making their hearts merry, behold, the men of the city, base fellows, beset the house round about, beating on the door; and they said to the old man, the master of the house, "Bring out the man who came into your house, that we may

know him." And the man, the master of the house, went out to them and said to them, "No, my brethren, do not act so wickedly; seeing that this man has come into my house, do not do this vile thing." …But the men would not listen to him. So the man (the house guest) seized his concubine and put her out to them; and they knew her, and abused her all night until the morning. And as dawn began to break, they let her go.

Leviticus 18:2
You shall not lie with a man as with a woman. It is an abomination.

Leviticus 20:13
If a male lies with a male as with a woman, both of them have committed an abomination; they shall be put to death, their blood is upon them.

Deuteronomy 23:18
You shall not bring the hire of a harlot, or the wages of a sodomite into the house of the Lord your God in payment for any vow; for both of these are an abomination to the Lord your God.

Romans 1:26, 27
For this reason God gave them up to dishonorable passions. Their women exchanged natural realtions for unnatural, and the men likewise gave up natural relations with women and were consumed with passion for one another, men committing shameless acts with men and receiving in their own persons the due penalty for their error.

1 Corinthians 6:9, 10
Do you not know that the unrighteous will not inherit the Kingdom of God? Do not be deceived; neither the immoral, nor idolators, nor adulteres, nor sexual perverts, nor thieves,

nor the greedy, nor drunkards, nor revilers, nor robbers will inherit the kingdom of God.

1 Timothy 1:8-10
Now we know that the law is good, if anyone uses it lawfully, understanding this, that the law is not laid down for the just but for the lawless and disobedient, for the ungodly and sinners, for the unholy and profane, for murderers of fathers and murderers of mothers, for manslayers, immoral persons, sodomites, kidnappers, liars, perjurers, and whatever else is contrary to sound doctrine.

"Christ" Checks

Church Leaders

- Does each decision that you make for your congregation meet God's vision for the church?
- Does your decisions revolve around where *you* would like to see your church or congregation going?
- Do you teach sermons based off God's word?
- Do you add some of your own personal thoughts or
- man-made traditions?
- Do you think as a leader of a congregation that you are pre-paring your members for Christ's return?
- Are you teaching against sin on the basis of holiness or hell?
- Are you creating disciples?

Church Members

- Are you faithful to the things of the church (attendance, finances, ministry, etc.)?
- Do you embrace new members with love and kindness?
- Are you friendly toward guests?

- If someone dresses in what you think is inappropriate attire for church, how do you treat that person?
- Why did you choose the church you attend?
- Do you think your leader is preparing you for Christ return?
- If Christ returned today, do you think you would go back with him? Why or Why not?

Dear God,

I know the church is your fortress and city of refuge. The church is the one object upon which you bestow your supreme regard. It is the theater of your grace, in which you delight to reveal your power to transform hearts. God, I know that there have been times when I completely lost focus on your purpose for the church and used it for my own hidden agenda. Lord, I know this has caused many to walk away from the church. I have allowed *sin* into your house.

Forgive me for my disobedience, pride, greed, and whatever else you see that is wrong in the church. But, as of this day going forth, I choose to remove myself from it. It is not about my personal agenda or me. It is all about you, Lord.

Lord, help me to get back on track to establish your kingdom and not mine. *And I tell you that you are Peter, and on this rock I will build my church, and the gates of Hades will not overcome it* (Matthew 16:18).

Chapter 2

Where is "Christ" in the Saints?

Saints are those whose hearts have been changed by Christ and who seek diligently to walk according to the dwelling of my spirit. Saints are separate from the world. They are "the salt of the earth." *Ye are the salt of the earth: but if the salt have lost his savior, wherewith shall it be salted? it is thenceforth good for nothing, but to be cast out, and to be trodden under foot of men* (Matthew 5:13 KJV).

Saints are "the light of the world." *"Ye are the light of the world. A city that is set on a hill cannot be hid"* (Matthew 5:14 KJV). They are created in my image. Saints are doers of my word, not just listeners. *"But be ye doers of the word, and not hearers only, deceiving your own selves"* (James 1:22 KJV). Where am I, my children? Do you have my spirit dwelling inside of you? Have you been baptized in my name? Many of you call yourselves a Christian, but I don't see anything about you that reflects my presence.

When my children have my spirit dwelling in them, there should be a real heart transformation. I purge them and create a clean heart of flesh. "And I will give them singleness of heart and put a new spirit within them. I will take away their stony, stubborn heart and give them a tender, responsive heart" (Ezekiel 11:19 NLT). The hearts should be tender and compassionate. They should always be willing to love, forgive, and help with pure motives.

For example, Christians must show love not just half of the time, but all of the time. I love you so much that I gave my only begotten son. *"For God so loved the world that he gave his only begotten Son, that whosoever believeth in him should not perish, but have everlasting life"* (John 3:16 KJV). I ask that you love one another and have compassion one for another as I do you. *"Finally, be ye all of one mind, having compassion one of another, love as brethren, be pitiful, be courteous"* (1Peter 3:8 KJV).

Instead, you do the opposite of what I ask. You, my children, walk around hating each other and are often envious, jealous, and angry toward one another. These negative emotions cause a great division in the body of Christ, and I am not pleased. Some of my children bring confusion and strife into my house. For these very reasons, souls are not brought into the kingdom of God. These disruptions break my heart as they overshadow my efforts to showcase the profound love I have for my children.

The attitude of some of my children is just as bad as or worse than the non-Christians. Some only show their Christ-like qualities on Sunday morning when they gather around other saints. It hurts me when I hear the world mocking my children, saying the saints are losing their respect. My children, how can you help anyone if you are not good examples? For some individuals, you might be the only Bible they ever see. The name "Christian" is used too loosely. Some so-called Christians don't seem to understand the meaning or the responsibility that comes with proclaiming that name. A Christian is a spiritually born-again person who professes to be a follower of Jesus Christ. Such a person exemplifies the teachings and the life of Jesus.

Furthermore, a Christian believes he has been unconditionally redeemed of his sins and has received eternal life in Christ by faith. It is a shame that some of my children take living for me so lightly. Saints are created in my image. Yet, many are not living lives that reflect the true life of Christ. The behaviors of professed Christians have caused people to stay away from churches within their communities. The rudeness and arrogance of some Christians have hindered unbelievers from growing closer to me. Some believers are very judgmental and often focus their attention on the outer appearance of a person instead of trying to win that individual's soul for the kingdom. In fact, it is often something as simple as an insincere attitude that causes some unbelievers to run back to the world where they feel less judged and more loved.

Saints are bringing a lot of their worldly ways into my house. Some saints have the audacity to be jealous of the ministries and spiritual gifts of their fellow church members. There is no need for any of my children to be jealous of one another. I am not a respecter of persons. *Wherefore now let the fear of the Lord be upon you; take heed and do it: for there is no iniquity with the Lord our God, nor respect of persons, nor taking of gifts* (2 Chronicles 19:7 KJV). What I do for one, I will do for another. You were all created with a purpose. If you seek me, then I will reveal to you the things you are destined to do. Everything that you do for the building of my kingdom is of the same importance in my eyes. There is no position greater than another, so do not envy anyone for their position or gift. Positions and talents are not yours to claim or to become boastful of. Please do not be proud and think that it is you who is performing. You are just my servants. I use you to get things done here on Earth. *These six things doth the Lord hate: yea, seven are an abomination unto him: A proud look, a lying tongue, and hands that shed innocent blood, (at these three—a heart the devises wicked schemes, Feet that are swift in running to mischief, A false witness who utters lies, And he who sows discord among brothers* (Proverbs 6:16-19 KJV).

There is an enormous need for willing vessels in the body of Christ. I need people who are not afraid to go to battle for my name's sake. Why is there such a lack of laborers in the body of Christ? There are many people claiming me as their Lord, but no one is willing to work for me. When I look around, I see that the churches are full every Sunday. But once you have what you want from me, you go on without sharing my word with someone else. Those who are willing to work for me are heavily judged and criticized for their past mistakes. Their peers find fault in them and criticize them for their willingness. Bombarded by so many stipulations and guidelines, it's no wonder that some of my children lose their desire. I am not happy with this. *Where am I?*

Why are some of my children so eager to tear each other down instead of building each other up? I have asked my children to pray for one another and lift each other up. *"Confess your faults one to another, and pray one for another, that ye may be healed. The effectual fervent prayer of a righteous man availeth much"* (James 5:16 KJV). If you think your brother in Christ is not adhering to my will, then rebuke him in love and keep him in prayer. How can we expect the world to love and respect my word when the saints do not? Where are the real saints? Where are the saints who are not afraid to stand up and proclaim Jesus Christ as Lord? Where are the saints who are still seeking God in the midnight hour in prayer? Where are the saints who still believe in living a holy and sanctified life? Where are the saints who will intercede for the brothers in Christ instead of backstabbing or slandering their name? It is hard enough to face the world when you are struggling. To have to fight against the brethren makes it more difficult. As my children, you should be willing to give up yourselves to help another saint in need. You never know when you will need someone to help you pull through a situation.

What happened to the "giving" saints? At one time, saints were people who gave all they had. If you are living your lives after me, you should be willing to give before anything else. I have blessed you so that you can be a blessing to others. The body cannot grow as a whole if one person does not have the resources. Share with someone who is in need. It is better to give than to receive. You should not store up things here on Earth because they will not last. *"Lay not up for yourselves treasures upon earth, where moth and rust doth corrupt, and where thieves break through and steal"* (Matthew 6:19 KJV). But, do store heavenly things. If your brother is in need, give him what he needs. *"And the King shall answer and say unto them, Verily I say unto you, Inasmuch as ye have done it unto one of the least of these my brethren, ye have done it unto me"* (Matthew 25:40 KJV). I will reward you for helping those in need.

I have asked each of you to carry each other's burdens. *"Bear ye one another's burdens, and so fulfill the law of Christ"* (Galatians 6:2 KJV). If one is down, the other should lift him up. Show compassion toward each other. Be willing to neglect yourself to help someone else. The abundance of love we have should overtake any evil. Our presence should bring peace in the midst of confusion. I have called you to be the peacemakers to the world that knows no peace. Invest your time into the things I stand for so that I can prepare you to be able to bless someone else's life. There are so many of my children who are hurting and need a word of encouragement, a hug, or just to know someone cares. But some of my saints are so selfish and wrapped up into their own worlds that they cannot reach out to help anyone else. Some of you are too busy with your careers, seeking a husband or wife, etc.

It saddens me that some of my children are walking around lost and have no one to trust or show concern. These are everyday people walking around lost, with no one to listen or to embrace. Where are the saints? The saints should be a liaison in my mission to win them over. Instead, the saints are sitting in the church pews talking about what the woman sitting a couple of seats ahead is wearing. The brothers are trying to dress up to see if they can find a wife or a weak sister with whom they can start a relationship. Meanwhile, Satan is sending his attackers to devour as many of my children as he can.

Saints are not on the frontline doing my work as they should be. As my children, it is your duty to tell the world how I have changed and blessed you abundantly. Saints should be vigilant in their mission to tell unsaved individuals that I can deliver them. There is no problem too big or small that I cannot fix. *"I am the Alpha and the Omega, and the ending, saith the Lord, which is, and which was, and which is to come, the Almighty"* (Rev. 1:8 KJV). I am challenging you, saints, to live uprightly so the world can see the "Christ" in you. I want them to see that I have changed that "old" man and create a "new" creature. *"Therefore if any man be in Christ, he is a new creature: old things are passed away; behold all things are become new"* (2 Corinthians 5:17 KJV). You have to be careful at all times about where you go and how you carry yourself (for example, this means that saints should not be in casinos, even if you are not gambling).

You should not let your good be evilly spoken of. *"Shew the very sight of evil"* (Romans 14:16 KJV). You should not be anywhere that would shame you if I came back that day. You should separate yourselves from the rest of the world (2 Corinthians. 6:17 KJV). The lives of the saints should let the world know what they stand for. A saint should not have to tell people that he is a child of God. If you are a true saint of God and are taking up your cross daily, your light should shine. There is a responsibility when you take up the cross. You have to love everybody and be kind to one another, *"Loving kindness have I drawn"* (Jeremiah 31:3b KJV). Love draws people to Christ. Your attitude toward people reflects on me; so when you say "Christ" is in you but you are mean, rude, or impatient, you are misrepresenting me. *"He who does not love does not know God, for God is love "*(1 John 4:8 NKJV).

The world is looking to see a resemblance of me in my children. They come for help and are not given the type of treatment they expect. They are shown a very rude and non-compassionate attitude that makes them turn away. You are blessed and have the means to be a blessing to someone else. Show love and kindness, and be sincere in your works. People are hurting and need someone to encourage them. Daily in this world is death and destruction. The world is not taught how to cast their cares to me. They get stressed, depressed, and burdened. This leads to sickness, disease, and early death. I am calling for my children to be that ear to listen, to intercede in prayer and encourage. Speak life into their dead situations and give them the boost they need to seek me and continue on with life.

You have to die to yourself and take up the cross daily. I ask you to share with others the things I have done in your life. Now that things are going good for you, I see a lack in praise and consistency in prayer. You used to worship and praise me with everything you had. You didn't worry about what people thought about you. Nowadays, it seems like the more I bless you, the weaker your praises become. Have you forgotten all that I have done for you? I am the one who has delivered you from drugs and alcoholism. I opened doors to help you get that good job and protected you from that tragedy that could have taken your life.

I healed your bodies and saved your lost, sinful souls. Praise me like you did when you needed me. I want you to praise me when things are good or bad. Praise brings deliverance in the midst of any situation, but praise along with prayer can open up heaven. Where are you, the praying saints? Prayer is a critical part of being a child of mine. Prayer is the primary way to communicate and build a personal relationship with me. When you spend time with me, you grow stronger in the Holy Spirit and are able to intercede for others. Saints in leadership roles should seek me, the Lord, now more than ever. You are not only praying and seeking me for yourself, but you also have souls for which you are accountable for. Prayer should always be a part of your daily life. How can I effectively reach my children if the leaders are not tuned into my message? My children's souls need to be fed spiritually. This is going to help them perfect their walk with me. Leaders, to really break strongholds and loosen bondages among your congregations, urge them to fast along with praying.

Encourage the saints to rediscover the hunger they once had for me, the times when they prayed and worshipped me for hours. These days, if church services last more than a couple of hours, some people become antsy; others leave. I often find myself asking my children, "Am I not the same God now as I was back then? What has caused you to lose interest in me?" At what point did you begin to have hang-ups and set limitations on how you will praise me? I am appalled when I see some of my so-called saints turning their noses up at fellow Christians for shouting with confidence that I am their Lord. Their praises are apparently too loud for some. It appears as though some so-called saints are afraid to fellowship with people who praise me with spirit and truth. *"God is a Spirit: and they that worship him must worship him in spirit and in truth"* (John 4:24 KJV). Whenever my real children attend a church-related event and scream or cry as they are celebrating me, I often hear some people say, "It does not take all of that." Have I not done so much for you that you should not mind celebrating me? I want my children to encourage each other to *"praise me with the timbrel and dance: praise me with stringed instruments and organs"*(Psalms 150:4 KJV). *"Make a joyful noise unto the Lord, all ye lands"* (Psalms 100:1 KJV).

Saints, it is time to take me "out of a box." Stop pulling me out at certain times and around certain people to make you look good. You are not supposed to be so worried about pleasing people. Some of you have one foot in the church and the other one in the world. You drink, party, and fornicate without any thought that what you are doing is wrong. But you are a devout Christian on Sundays. These kinds of people are what I call my "Sunday Saints." *"You can not love God and mammoth, you either love one or hate the other one"* (Matthew 6:24 KJV). I do not like a lukewarm saint. I will spit you out (Rev.3:16 KJV). I am left wondering, "Why are my children shying away from me? What is keeping them from loving me with all their heart? Why are they limiting the time they devote to studying the scripture?" I am just a convenience for some of you. When your lives are going well, I am not needed. Some of you go weeks without communicating (praying) with me or thanking me for life itself. I notice that I am always at the bottom of your list of priorities.

The saints take me for granted, as if I have to breathe life into your sinful bodies. Although I am frequently ignored, I am a patient and very merciful God who desires all of my children to come to me before it is too late. I always protect my children from any hurt, harm, and danger. I am constantly providing for your daily needs. Nonetheless, I am still rejected. After all I have done, many of my children still allow Satan to keep them so occupied that they do not have time to pray, read the word, or minister the gospel to the lost. Saints are becoming relaxed. They think they've arrived. Some people think there is no need to hunger for the things of God. Some of my children do not see a need to change from their sinful ways. Some would rather attend services that make them feel good and not con-victed. Many non-Christians do not like to attend a service where leaders challenge their sinful nature.

Even some saints dislike these types of services; their spirit is not comfortable. They feel uneasy and exposed. Even though some of my children ignore me, I will never give up on saving their souls. I will do whatever it takes to get your attention. I am here for you. Come to me, my children, while there is still time. Once it is over, it's over. There will be no second chance to make it right. Your soul will spend eternity either in heaven or hell. Children, please stop trying to fool me because I am everywhere, and I know everything, including what is in your heart. Please, my children, turn from your wicked ways and live according to my word. You will have to give account to me for everything you have done one day.

For we must all appear before the judgment seat of Christ; that every one may receive the things done in his body, according to that he hath done, whether it be good or bad (2 Corinthians 5:10 KJV).

"Christ" Checks

1. Are you fulfilling God's purpose for your life?
2. Do you treat people the way Christ desires you to?
3. Do you help the needy and the poor?
4. What does it mean that a believer in Christ becomes a "new creation"?
5. What really changes?
6. Why do you still sin?
7. Since you became a Christian, what are some "new" things in your own life?

Dear God,

I know that you have a certain expectation of me as your child. I am supposed to be light in the midst of darkness and the salt of the Earth. Instead, I am living the life of someone who is lost. I am blending in with the darkness, and I sometimes have to ask, "Am I what Christ died for? Am I portraying an image that allows others to see you in me?" Lord, I need a refreshing of your Spirit to come in and make me new again. I sometimes feel I am losing the battle. I know that is a trick from the enemy. I know that I will have victory. Please do not give up on me. Continue to guide me into my destiny and give me wisdom and knowledge to fulfill it. Lord, wherever I have fallen short, please rebuild that area in my life. Help me to be the sample saint for the world to see. I am rededicating my life to you, Lord.

Chapter 3

Where Is "Christ" in the Workplace?

A workplace is a place (whether or not within or forming part of a building, structure, or vehicle) where any person works for gain or reward under the control of an employer. At any workplace, I expect my children to be model employers and employees. They should *always* approach each task as if they were doing it for me. *"Teach slaves to be subject to their masters in everything, to try to please them, not to talk back to them"* (Titus 2:9 KJV). Colleagues of my children should be impressed by their high level of professionalism and humbleness and desire to follow suit. They should also know, without a shadow of the doubt, that I am the primary reason for all of the successes of my children. However, it is becoming increasingly difficult to find people who will give me just a little credit for their job security, pay raises, etc.

Instead, I find many who like to praise themselves for their talents and endurance. *Where am I?*

It was me who gave some of today's most celebrated entrepreneurs the very ideas that spawned their multibillion-dollar companies. Yet, I am still waiting to be recognized. It saddens me when I think about the high number of people who believe it was they alone who created these so-called "groundbreaking" inventions. Even more insulting, leaders of some of these companies seem to be inspired by greed along with the mistreatment of my children. I am disturbed when various leaders use their employees to become rich and then seek ways to sabotage these workers or make them feel inferior. The number of people in positions of power who thrive off the fear factor is astounding. Also, many company owners apparently have no thought for their employees' current mental or financial state as some deny their employees the basic benefits needed to survive while they live lavish lifestyles. Despite the accumulation of enough wealth to take care of their families for generations to come, some employers continue to work my children long hours, keeping them from enjoying the fruits of *their* labor.

These CEOs are so greedy that they make their employees work on Sunday—the day I have set aside for rest and a day when many of my children come to my house for worship. *And he said unto them, this is that which the Lord hath said; Tomorrow is the rest of the holy Sabbath unto the Lord: bake that which ye will bake to day, and seethe that ye will seethe; and that which remaineth over lay up for you to be kept until the morning* (Exodus 16:23 KJV).

Why do employers continue to take advantage of my children for their personal gain? Why do they continue to be greedy and store up riches here on Earth? *"For what is a man profited, if he shall gain the whole world, and lose his own soul? Or what shall a man give in exchange for his soul"* (Matthew 16:26 KJV)? My children, riches cannot buy paradise everywhere. (Read the story about Lazarus and the beggar in Luke 16:19-31 KJV.)

Once you leave this world, your money is worthless. Greed is one of the main reasons why a lot of companies fail. While gloating over a supposed iron-clad budget, they manage to overlook the fact that they have hired other greedy people to manage their business. As a result, they end up losing everything. Devastating experiences such as these could be avoided if people would just seek me first. *"Seek ye first the kingdom of God and all his righteousness and he will direct your path"* (Matthew 6:33 KVJ). I should always be at the forefront of every plan or idea. It's a shame that more people refuse to seek my help when I can, with a snap of a finger, send unique ideas, lucrative business deals, and stellar employees. If only my children would let me be their guide and allow me to order their steps. *Where am I?*

Marketplace Ministry

Many of my children have a fear of witnessing to their coworkers and friends. My gospel needs to go to the marketplace. This is where most of my children are during the week. They spend more time at work then they do with their families or in church. This is a prime place to minister to my children by showing love or sharing the gospel. There are seven reasons you should take ministry to work.

Reason number one: Almost all non-Christians are in the marketplace.

Today, less than 20% of Americans attend church regularly. In many European countries, the percentages are much lower. At the current rate, regular church attendance is projected to drop to 11.7% by 2050. The good news is that these people who aren't attending the church will still be waking up to go to work alongside their Christian coworkers in the marketplace each morning.

Reason number two: Almost all Christians are in the marketplace.

At least 85% of the Christian workforce spends 60-70% of their waking hours in the marketplace. In addition to serving our families and our local churches, the marketplace is the primary context in which our spiritual gifts should be used. The ministry potential for Christians using their spiritual gifts collaboratively in the marketplace is astounding!

Reason number three: Discipleship actually can happen in the marketplace.

Church leaders often are criticized for the lack of discipleship and spiritual growth among their congregations. Let's give our pastors a break. How much discipleship can actually happen during a two-hour church service on Sunday?

Discipleship—that is, becoming more like Jesus—happens in everyday life. Yes, discipleship can happen anywhere...even during a two-hour, lecture-style event on Sunday. However, the potential for discipleship and ministry investment in a weekly service is a fraction of what is possible during an entire work-week spent with our co-workers, clients, etc.

Reason number four: The marketplace is a more authentic showroom of Christianity.

If you were shopping for a car, you'd probably go to a showroom. Before you bought anything, you'd probably want to see if the car actually functions properly on the road. You might even ask the dealer to allow you to take the car home for a day or two to test it out.

The local church is like the showroom for Christianity. The marketplace is the test drive. The marketplace is where our unbelieving coworkers get to see if they really want what we have. Daily, they see how we react under pressure. They see how we treat people. They see how much God truly matters to us in our daily lives.

As mentioned in the first reason, most people aren't even coming to the "showroom" anymore, so marketplace Christians are now serving as both the showroom and the test drive of Christianity.

Reason numbe five: The marketplace forces the Church to use all of its capabilities.

Personality-driven and super-pastor Christianity doesn't work in the marketplace. Having a bunch of Christians sitting on the sidelines of ministry may not prevent a local church from increasing numerically, but it won't transform the marketplace for the glory of God.

So far, most of the teaching about "marketplace ministry" has been defining marketplace ministry without regard for people's unique spiritual gifts. For example, if I have an apostolic gift, of course I'm going to view marketplace ministry as a mandate to "ascend and take the Business Mountain for God." If I have a pastoral gift (i.e., marketplace chaplains), of course, I'm going to view marketplace ministry as a calling to "care for the personal needs of my employees and/or coworkers."

We need to approach marketplace ministry in a way that leverages the spiritual gifts of all Christians in the marketplace. The one-size-fits-all approach only produces self-condemnation and ineffectiveness for marketplace Christians attempting to operate outside of their God-given spiritual gifts.

Reason number six: Denominational divisions are less-destructive in the marketplace.

We can choose whether to attend a Baptist church, Pentecostal-Charismatic church, Presbyterian church, a nonddenominational Church, etc., but most of us don't have the luxury of coworking only with Christians with whom we agree theologically. The marketplace has a way of diluting some of these differences. This opens the door to collaborative ministry beyond the walls of our local churches and traditions.

Reason number seven: Everything gets funded from the marketplace.

All money comes from value that has been created in the marketplace, and business professionals ultimately decide what gets funded. These business professionals need to know God and His plans for their lives in order to make righteous decisions concerning money. Although business is often thought of only as the economic engine of the Church, I hope that we will begin to see and realize its full potential for transforming society for the glory of God.

I hope after reading the above article. You will see that marketplace ministry is an area that is ripe for sharing the gospel. For those of you who do believe in my power, it's time to stop being timid and become the leader I have inspired you to be. Stop sitting on your talents! It's time to stop listening to dream killers who negatively speak against that brilliant idea that I have impressed upon you. If you continue to believe them and not me, you will never fulfill the purpose I have given you. *"Eyes hath not seen nor ears heard the great things that God have for those that love him"* (1 Corinthians 2:9 KJV). If I am the creator of all things and have all the riches at my fingertips, why would I not want to share it with my children? There is no government system that can take care of my children the way I can. All I am seeking is your trust.

Seven Mountain Mandate

In order to truly transform any nation with the Gospel of Jesus Christ, these seven facets of society must be reached: religion, family, education, government, media, arts and entertainment, and business. I have been speaking through my prophet to inform you of the need to go into these areas. There should not be an area where my presence is not known.

1. Religion

Every society has some type of belief in a superior being or beings. In the east, religions tend to be polytheistic (many gods) or outright idolatrous (such as Hinduism and Buddhism). Although these religions are thousands of years old, they nonetheless continue to thrive today. In the West, Christianity and Catholicism are predominant, but postmodern views are increasingly being accepted and the concept of God is being rejected. This is especially true in Europe.

The Christian church is described in the Greek language as the ecclesia. Literally translated, the word ecclesia means "governing body." Although we don't condone theocracies, this translation suggests that the church should have great influence in all other spheres that make up a society. With a plethora of categorized religions around the world, it's the church's responsibility to reach the lost with the love and gospel of Jesus Christ and expand the kingdom in ministerial efforts, both nationally and internationally.

2. Family

In any functional society, the family is the "building block" of the community. Throughout the Bible, you will find familial examples that portray how we ought to live our lives today. God desires that men, women, and children within a family be united as one in His love. After all, He is the ultimate Father (Romans 8:14-17).

The families of the United States have been under constant and prolonged attack. Today, the assailants are fatherlessness, divorce (50% rate in secular and Christian marriages), abuse, homosexual marriage, pornography, and other negative influences have brought great dysfunction to American life. God is calling fathers and mothers (both spiritual and biological) to bring order to the chaos that the enemy has unleashed against families in America. He also wants to bring healing to marriages and relationships within families in order to maintain a moral foundation for children in the future to stand upon.

3. Education

At one time, the education system of America unapologetically incorporated the Bible, prayer to the God of the Bible, and Biblical values in every aspect of school life. Not coincidentally, this system produced a people who produced the most powerful and prosperous nation the Earth has ever seen.

Now, the children of our nation are inundated with liberal ideologies, atheistic teaching, and postmodern principles in our public schools and in most universities (including many Christian institutions). Put simply; they are being indoctrinated with often false, biased, and anti-Biblical information.

A reintroduction of biblical truth and Bible-centric values is the key to renewal and restoration in America's failing educational system.

4. *Government*

Proverbs 14:34 states that "righteousness exalts a nation, but sin is a reproach to any people." Many times, as exemplified in the Old Testament, a nation's moral standards are dependent on those exhibited by its leaders (or predominant political party). While each individual is responsible for his or her own sins, the fact remains that people are greatly influenced by those moral (or lack thereof) that popular leaders adopt.

The progressive liberal agenda, empowered by well-known men and women in the arts and entertainment industries, have made significant gains in the political arena over the past few decades. In fact, many liberal groups, seek to remove anything related to God or Christianity from the governmental and educational systems because of a misapplied interpretation of the phrase, "separation of church and state." We must see a shift in this arena in order to preserve the Christian heritage that America was founded upon. The goal is to put in place righteous political leaders that will positively affect all aspects of government.

5. *Media*

The media mountain includes news sources such as radio, TV news stations, newspapers, Internet news and opinion (blog) sites, etc. The media has the potential to sway popular opinion on current issues based upon its reporting, which is not always truthful or accurate. In recent elections, the liberal "elite" media played a vital role. Their generally supportive and positive reporting greatly influenced the outcome.

There has been a rise in Christian news services, which is needed. However, to bring transformation to the mountain of media, Christians who are gifted for and called into this type of work must be willing to report righteously and truthfully in the secular marketplace.

6. *Arts and Entertainment*

In this mountain, we find some of the most influential forces shaping our society. Music, filmmaking, television, social media, and the performing arts drive the cultural tastes, values, and standards of a nation's citizens, particularly its youth.

With a heavy reliance on the strong appeal of sex, drugs, and alcohol, the arts and entertainment industries wield significant influence. The body of Christ needs powerful, righteous men and women who are not afraid to take their God-given talent into the arts and entertainment arenas. People ready to further His purposes while impacting those who are lost in darkness and would not otherwise be interested in any kind of Christian message in traditional forms.

7. *Business*

The ability to literally create wealth through ingenuity, enterprise, creativity, and effort is a God-given gift and a universal impulse. The markets and economic systems that emerge whenever people are free to pursue buying and selling become the lifeblood of a nation. This includes anything from farms to small businesses to large corporations.

Of course, this realm is prone to corruption through idolatry, greed, and covetousness. In response, the church must embrace its responsibility to train up those who are called into the marketplace to manage businesses and provide leadership with integrity and honesty. We believe it is the Lord's will to make his people prosperous, and He desires for His Church to use its wealth to finance the work of kingdom expansion. Simply put, prosperity with a purpose.

There is a great need for marketplace ministry. I have listed some reasons why it is needed. I have also listed some areas. Now, I just need you to step out on faith to start to go into those areas. "And then he told them, "Go into all the world and preach the Good News to everyone" (Mark 16:15).

Trust me and see just how far you'll go. It is obvious how desperately I am needed in the workplace, but I can't make a difference if you don't invite me there. So, children, don't be afraid to share the gospel with your bosses, coworkers, and anyone else you come in contact with. If you stand up, things will change for the better. Just think about how good the workplace would be if everybody in your office was saved, blood washed, and filled with the Holy Ghost. You would have a peaceful work environment.

There would be no gossiping about each other. Everybody would work together to complete job assignments and share knowledge among each other. Doing an honest and good job would be all it took to get a promotion or raise. There would be no lying or performing dishonest deeds to get favoritism from your boss. There will be no discrimination because of race, age or education level. Also, allowing me in the workplace will cause less financial stress on the bosses, which would in return lessen the stress on you.

I could create Godly characters within the workplace resulting in less company fraud. This type of environment would make *all* bosses and employees desire to work and give 110%. Then, companies would get great revenues, and stocks would exceed expectations. This could cause a ripple effect, as companies would begin paying employees their true worth and give them good benefits packages. They would show employees that they are an important component of the company and its success. This type of environment would be stress-free, resulting in less sickness and bad attitudes. Employees would take less time off for being sick and there would not be a need for so many different types of medical plans. This alone could save companies millions of dollars. You, my children, could enjoy this and much more by just allowing my presence to come into your workplace.

My presence can also thwart a lot of the immoral conduct that goes on, such as marital affairs, sexual harassment cases, and job-related assaults. It is important to remember that whenever you take me out, the devil comes in and creates the opposite of what my presence would bring. When Satan is in charge, employees are out for long periods of time on sick leave, rehabilitation from drugs or alcohol, or everything else under the sun. Some who are fired from their jobs leave and then return to kill or wound the person who mistreated them along with innocent bystanders. They are devastated as they believed their job was the only source of income for them and their families. If you allow me to come in, I can change the hearts and minds of people like this by giving them hope and faith regardless of any situation. *"I came that they may have life and more abundantly"* (John 10:10b, KJV).

I have provided more than enough reasons why employees should encourage prayer and Christian organizations in the workplace. Hearing my words and releasing your burdens in prayer help to reduce stress. Stress is a silent killer that leads to strokes, heart attacks, and other life-threatening diseases. Why leave someone out of your life who can heal you of any sickness or infirmities? Someone who can direct your path and create a life that does not have these kinds of problems? Your life would be peaceful, full of joy, and prosperous. I am the creator of all things. Seek me, and the returns on your investments will be far better than any the stock market could produce. I urge you to put your trust in me and let me direct you into a good life here on Earth as well as a wonderful eternal life in heaven. Let me place you in a win-win situation. *"Whatever is loosed in heaven will be loosed on earth"* (Matthew 16:19b, KJV). There is no poverty in heaven, and it should be the same on Earth. If you, as my children, apply the word to your lives, you would get the same results.

You have nothing to lose but everything to gain. Pray daily about every decision. Search the scriptures, and see how all the people in the Bible were blessed. They overcame unbelievable obstacles by simply believing in me. They kept my commandments and allowed me to order their steps. I did it for them and want to do it for you. While I have access to all the riches and gold, I desire to have a personal relationship with you. Worship and glorify me at work, just like you do around the saints on Sundays. Do not be afraid to go into a quiet place and seek me when things get rough. While working on a project that you cannot do, seek me so that I can give you the wisdom to complete the task or put someone in your pathway that will help you. Never put a limit on what I can do in your life. I am your Father and will never leave you nor forsake you (Hebrew 13:5b, KJV). I will direct your path, as I know what is best for you. I will teach you to have total faith in me and give you the patience to allow me to work hardships out for you. From now on, do not move before I tell you or allow the devil to trick you with his temptations. If you heed my advice, you will never miss out on what I have in store for you. You need to focus on the treasures above and not those treasures here on Earth. If you let me be the head of your company, there is no trial you cannot conquer.

Christ does not care about titles, and there is no position that is greater than any other in my eyes. You will not have to worry about a benefit plan or a 401K when you retire. I will take care of you. I have the best retirement plan anybody could ever want. *"But he that received seed into the good ground is he that heareth the word, and understandeth it; which also beareth fruit, and bringeth forth, some an hundredfold, some sixty, some thirty"* (Matthew 13:23 KJV). You will not have to worry about anything. If I am able to command ravens to feed one of my children in the wilderness. *"And it shall be that thou shalt drink of the brook; and I have commanded the ravens to feed thee there"* (I Kings 17:4 KJV). What I do for one, I will do for another. It disheartening to see how much trust some of you have put into the companies you work for. You get up daily, automatically expecting the building that houses your job will be standing and trusting that the company will continue to provide your paycheck week after week. Why can you not trust me like this, the one who created the company and provided you with the jobs?

But, I guess I am just not good enough for some of you. You would rather continue to trust the companies, some of whom will soon close, downsize, and restructure and will replace your position with another one, than place your faith in me. As usual, regardless of how disloyal some of you have been, I will never let you go. For my faithful followers, please continue to worship me in the workplace. Continue to be model bosses and employees by performing your duties above and beyond what is expected. Continue to stand out from the crowd when it comes to your work ethics and behavior. Continue to show your colleagues how dependable and trustworthy you are. Continue to obey all policies, laws and procedures within the work environment. *Servants, be obedient to them that are your masters according to the flesh, with fear and trembling, in singleness of your heart, as unto Christ; Not with eye service, as men pleasers; but as the servants of Christ, doing the will of God from the heart; With good will doing service, as to the Lord, and not to men: Knowing that whatsoever good thing any man doeth, the same shall he receive of the Lord, whether he be bond or free. And, ye masters, do the same things unto them, forbearing threatening: knowing that your Master also is in heaven; neither is there respect of persons with him* (Ephesian 6:5-9 KJV).

Let them know that I, Jehovah Jireh (Provider), can supply all things for my children. Do not be selfish; share my greatness with others. I want the entire world to know of my love and mercy. Remember, there is no environment your God cannot improve. But, you have to invite me in, as I do not go anywhere I am not wanted. *Where am I?*

Christ" Checks

Employers

- Employers do you treat your workers fairly (Ephesians 6:5-9).
- Do you give fair wages to all of your workers?
- Do you show partiality or favoritism toward certain workers?
- Do you provide a safe work environment for your employees?
- What decisions do you consider when hiring or firing an employee?

Employees

- From a scale from 1 to 10, how would you rate the stability of your company?
- Do you put all of your trust in your job for your daily provisions? (Matthew 6:25-34)
- Do you perform your job duties above and beyond expectation?
- Do your employer and colleagues respect you as a Christian?
- Have you set a good example of Christ in your place of work?
- Do you share the gospel with your colleagues?

Dear God,

I know that you are my Jehovah Jireh. I know that you provide all things, including my job. Lord, while I am working, I want to represent You in all ways. I want to be the model employee. My behavior and work ethics should be what employers look for in employees. I know I am not supposed to be a part of any gossip or un-Christ like conduct. Lord, remove the slothful spirit from me. I know You said in Your word, "If a man will not work, he shall not eat" (2 Thessalonians 3:10). I know that I am supposed to work to provide for my family. I should not take my employment lightly and do things that might cause me to lose it. Lord, not only does my ethics matter while at work, but they also have an effect on my children. They are reaping the benefits of the good decisions and suffering because of the bad. Oftentimes, my behavior is what they base their lives upon. Lord, help me as an employer to not to be greedy and take my employees for granted. Lord, help me to stay humble and always be grateful to You for giving me business ideas. Help me, Lord, to take You with me wherever I go. Help me to live what the word says while at work. Lord, I repent now of every slothful act and mistreatment of Your children for my own personal gain.

Bondservants, be obedient to those who are your masters according to the flesh, with fear and trembling, in sincerity of heart, as to Christ; not with eyeservice, as men-pleasers, but as bondservants of Christ, doing the will of God from the heart, with goodwill doing service, as to the Lord, and not to men, knowing that whatever good anyone does, he will receive the same from the Lord, whether he is a slave or free. And you, masters, do the same things to them, giving up threatening, knowing that your own Master also is in heaven, and there is no partiality with Him (Ephesians 6:5-9 NKJV).

Chapter 4

Where Is "Christ" in Schools?

Primary and secondary schools are institutions for the instruction of children under college-age. While attending school, a variety of subjects are taught in order for the children to receive a foundation of knowledge. The curriculum of the classes taken is based on the state requirements. After completing secondary school, students can decide to further their education by attending a college or trade school. At this level, schools attempt to give students the tools that will help them live a successful life. School is a place where what you learn can help prepare you for life, but you cannot learn about me (Christ). I am the creator of life. I am ruled out of the schools, where I can protect children. But when something tragic occurs, everyone asks, "How can God let this happen?" Remember, I was taken out of schools. In return, you allowed every foul spirit of the devil come into the schools. There are laws against praying to or mentioning my name because it offends someone else's religion or belief system. There is no other God but me.

There is *"one God and Father of all who is above all, and through all and in you all"* (Ephesians 4:6 KJV). Who are you offending? I am the one true living God. Children should be able to pray and say the name of Jesus anytime their hearts desire. When you keep children from learning about me, their thoughts will be replaced with the evil ways of the devil. Once the devil is in control, violence, drugs, and the pressures of life come into their spirit. They become disobedient and have little interest in getting an education. This type of behavior comes from the negative influences around them. What influences are you allowing to affect your kids? They do not have the privilege of a Godly influence because that door was closed. Now, your children are influenced by homosexuals, witchcraft, gangs, and drugs, instead of learning about me.

Children are vulnerable and feel lonely when they are away from the comfort of their safe home. They need a circle of people around them, so they can feel secure. There is no one who wants to be alone or considered unworthy of having friends. Children mock each other badly, causing many to have low self-esteem. Parents, please teach your children about me daily. Tell them it is proper to isolate yourself to keep from being in the midst of bad company, especially when other children or cliques at school are not embracing a Godly character. Parents, teach children to take me with them and tell them how much I love them and that *"I will never leave thee, nor forsake thee"* (Hebrew 13:5b). I want nothing but the best for their lives. I am here for whatever. I can help with their studies. I will keep their minds free from worrying about fitting into the social groups. Teach your children to love Christ and desire to live for me at an early age. Their lives will be blessed. I will protect them from anything the devil tries to use. There are spirits lurking within the halls and on the playgrounds of schools daily. They are looking for a body to reside in and a lonely, insecure person to join in their evilness. If they are not taught at home about Christ, how will they learn? They will think that evilness is the norm and get caught up in the devil's trap. I am asking, *"Where am I?"*

Why can't my name be said in schools? It brings peace, deliverance, and a sense of hope. There is constant complaining about the school systems' performance. Teachers are not dedicated to their students. Teachers cannot teach or embrace students because of their behavior, thus creating a disconnection between the two. The students start to think no one cares. They stop trying, and this causes them to receive a poor education and maybe even to drop out of school. They will not seek higher education to prepare themselves to get good jobs. As a result, many will become involved in illegal types of behavior or depend on the welfare system. I desire the best for my children just as every father should. Parents worry about their child's future and safety on a daily basis. With all the violence and poor education in some of the schools, parents begin to think the district is at fault and put their children in private schools. Some move to another area that is supposed to have a better school system, only to find problems that exist there as well. Have you tried Jesus? *Where am I?*

Another problem that is causing trouble in schools is alcoholism. This is one of the major spirits destroying children. This spirit is well known. It has been around for years. Students drink on a regular basis, and parents are unaware. They hide in the bathrooms during breaks drinking. Most of them drink before coming to school, and they picked up this behavior from another child while attending school. This is what children learn while away from their home, but no one is complaining about this enough to ban alcohol. How are underage children getting alcohol? They cannot get access to a Bible or say anything with "God" in it, but things that can destroy them are easily accessible. *Where am I?*

There are some serious consequences when dealing with this spirit. Alcohol is a drug. It alters your mind, body, and emotions. It is also our nation's largest youth drug problem, killing 6.5 times as many young people as all illicit drugs combined. Here are some more facts about alcohol. Alcohol is a leading cause of death among youth, particularly teenagers. It contributes substantially to adolescent motor vehicle crashes, other traumatic injuries, suicide, date rape, and family and school problems.

These statistics below hurts my heart as my babies can get access to things such as alcohol or drugs easier than a Bible.

Facts and Statistics on Alcohol Abuse in Teens:

- By eighth grade, almost 30% of kids have tried drinking alcohol.
- Fifty percent of sophomores have abused alcohol.

- Seventy-one percent of high school seniors have used alcohol.
- Twenty-three percent of twelfth graders reported on binge drinking—with over five drinks in a row.
- Eight percent of high school students admit to driving after drinking.
- Twenty-four percent of high-school students rode with a driver who had been drinking alcohol.
- Teenagers who drink alcohol are 50% more likely to try cocaine ("coke") than those who never use alcohol.
- Eleven percent of all alcohol consumed in the United States is from underage drinkers.
- The average age of a boy who tries alcohol is eleven; girls are on average thirteen.
- Teens that started drinking before the age of fifteen are five times more likely to become addicted to alcohol later on, unlike those kids who waited until after they were twenty-one.
- Teens that drink often are more than three times more likely to commit self-harm—such as cutting or suicide attempts—than teens that don't drink.
- Alcohol is the leading factor in the top three causes for death between fifteen and twenty-four year olds, causing auto crashes, homicides, and suicides.

In 2013, approximately 1.4 million people aged 12-20 engaged in heavy drinking, which is consuming five drinks or more on at least five occasions over the span of a month.

Facts and Statistics on Drug Abuse in Teens

- Almost 50% of high school seniors have abused a drug of some kind.
- By eighth grade 15% of kids have used marijuana.
- Fourty-three of high-school seniors have used marijuana.

- 8.6% of 12th graders have used hallucinogens—4% report on using LSD specifically.
- Over 60% of teens report that drugs of some kind are kept, sold, and used at their school.
- One in every nine high-school seniors has tried synthetic marijuana (also known as "Spice" or "K2").
- 1.3% of high school seniors have tried bath salts.
- 64% of teens say they have used prescription pain killers that they got from a friend or family member.
- 28% of teens know at least one person who has tried ecstasy.
- 7.6% of teens use the prescription drug Aderall.
- Over 5% of 12th graders have used cocaine and over 2% have used crack.
- More teenagers die from taking prescription drugs than the use of cocaine and heroin combined.

The pervasiveness of teenage alcohol and drug misuse is particularly worrisome given the association of teen drinking with accidents, suicide, violent behavior, high-risk sex, and emotional problems. Parents, communities, and governments have thus been justifiably intent on controlling teen alcohol consumption along with consumption of other drugs. But, the problems still exist and the numbers of users continue to increase. So once again, I am asking, *"Where am I?"* Christ is our Jehovah Nissi, your protector (Exodus 17:15, Jude 7:19-24). I want to protect the children from all harm. I can deliver them and break the strongholds that try to keep them bound. I should be allowed back into the schools. My spirit should walk the halls. Allow the spirit of the living God to run the devil out. You have tried your way. But violence and pregnancy keep increasing in the teenage population as well as sins such as homosexuality and lesbianism which people were once afraid to let be known.

They have become bold. Do you think the principals, teachers, or superintendents can keep this type of behavior out of the schools? If so, what are they waiting for? How many more kids have to drop out of school? How many more acts of violence have to take place? What else has to happen? If it can be fixed without me, then fix it. Children are being destroyed daily. Another event that has played a major role in the downward turn of the schools is the removal of prayer. There were a couple of decisions such as Engel v. Vitale (1961) and Abington School District v. Schempp (1963), the two landmark Supreme Court cases that effectively outlawed staff-sanctioned prayer in public schools. These laws decided that I am better in a box until Sunday mornings. Where have the schools gone since the decision? Did you get the result you expected to gain? Were Engel v. Vitale and Abington School District v. Schempp good decisions?

This decision was made almost forty years ago. Since that time, America has experienced radical decline in each of the four areas that the children's prayer touched upon: youth, family, education and national life. Children once prayed this simple prayer daily: *Almighty God we acknowledge our dependence on Thee and beg Thy blessing over us, our parents, our teachers and our nation.* This simple prayer blessed all areas that the children prayed for daily. There has been drastic change since the prayer was banned.

The enemy has attacked all these areas in a mighty way. The attack against children had a big impact. Children have a sinful nature and do not have to be taught how to sin. They came into this world as sinners. They need their mind renewed and transformed (Romans 12:2). Children need proper guidance. Children spend more time with their teachers and classmates during a day than with their parents. Parents should feel some sense of comfort from knowing that before their child's day begins, he has prayed for protection over himself, family, and country.

This should be something each parent wants. I know some parents pray with their kids at home. What about those that do not have any knowledge about me in their homes? The reason for the removal of prayer from our schools was a violation of the third commandment that tells us "not to take the name of the Lord in vain." Worse than taking the Lord's sacred name in vain is treating it with contempt, denying its rightful place and stripping it from public use and even from the lips of children. My word says, *"Let the little children come to Me, and do not forbid them"* (Mark 9:36-37).

Where are my Christian parents? You are allowing the governmental laws to hinder your child's life. Stand up and fight for Christ. I died for you but you cannot speak up for me and change this outdated decision. Stop allowing laws to use my word to bring destruction into your lives. My word is meant to bring change and hope for the good. When you use my name in vain, you blaspheme or use it in a vulgar way.

When an innocent child recognizes me, this is not using my name in "vain." This is love. Along with removing prayer, children cannot learn about me at school. Schools want to teach them about how the world was created without teaching them about the creator. Man cannot fully understand how the earth was formed. Can anyone explain how the water and land are divided and how the water stays in its place and does not come upon land until I command it? Can you explain how the days and nights are divided? The sun gives just enough heat for each season. There are different temperatures all over the world. You can be in different part of the world, in a different season and time zone. The reason is, *"The earth is the Lord's and the fullness thereof, the world and they that dwell there in"* (Psalms 24:1). There is no scientist that is knowledgeable enough to recreate anything that God created. Parents are there any concerns that children may not learn about me? If they are not being taught at home and their parents cannot afford to send them to the private Christian schools, they will never learn about me. *Where am I?*

I want children to know about the abundant love I have for them. Parents, teach them about Christ. I am more than just a Christmas or Easter program. Most children only hear about me on these days. They associate me with gifts or an Easter bunny. If they learn about sex, drugs, and violence in schools, why they cannot learn about me, their heavenly Father?

Learning about me is just as important as learning math or science. I will take them further than knowing these subjects alone could ever do. I can change their heart about joining a gang. I can clean their minds and keep them from the desire to steal, kill, or use drugs. I can teach them to wait until they are married to have sex. This would lead to a significantly drop in the number of teenage and unwed mothers. This will prepare them to become successful and teach their children about Christ's role in their life. Schools are teaching that it is okay to have sex as long as it is "safe sex." Are they grooming your children for sex? This is alright with parents. No one has banned it out of schools. The schools teach them to protect themselves from sexually transmitted diseases (STDs) and unplanned pregnancy by using a condom and birth control.

This is approved by the parents and the leaders of the school systems. They are not 100% correct in this. Statistics show 15% of sexually active women within a given year become pregnant if her partner uses a condom correctly and every time. The National Institute of Allergy and Infectious Diseases in America brought together 180 persons to discuss condom effectiveness (11). Of this group, a panel of 28 experts in the field prepared a report. Despite all the claims that have been made about condoms and "safer sex," all the studies that have been done and all of the published medical papers, the panel concluded that it was impossible to draw conclusions about the effectiveness of condoms in preventing HPV infections, genital herpes, syphilis, chancroid, gonorrhea, chlamydia, and trichomoniasis.

The use of birth control and other contraceptives is not 100% to stop pregnancy and comes with health risks. Some of the mild health risks of using birth control are as follows:

- Larger breasts
- Weight gain or loss
- Reduced or increased acne
- Slight nausea
- Emotional sensitivity right before your period
- Mood swings throughout your cycle
- Irregular bleeding or spotting
- Breast tenderness
- Decreased libido

The more serious side effects include the following:

- Increased risk of cervical and breast cancers
- Increased risk of heart attack and stroke
- Migraines
- Higher blood pressure
- Gall bladder disease
- Infertility
- Benign liver tumors
- Decreased bone density
- Yeast overgrowth and infection
- Increased risk of blood clotting

One of the things the world does is paint a false picture to make you think things are good. The enemy uses the worldly things to trap you. Lead your life to destruction at an early age. How can anyone consider taking birth control with all those side effects?

Also, the schools making it seem okay to have "protected sex," while the number of teenagers having sex is outrageous. Children being the irresponsible beings that they are do not always listen and started having unprotected sex, causing a lot of teenagers to have sexually transmitted diseases. They usually do not know they have it so they pass it on. Schools teaching children about sex has had no positive results. The children are learning about things that should not happen until they are married adults and only with their mates. In their teenage years, children learn how to have sex and how to start a family. While only being a teenager, they are not old enough to get a job to provide for the family. Why teach children about sex at a young age? Their minds are not mature or responsible enough to handle the results that can come from premarital sex. *Where am I?*

There is so much influence about sex and drugs on the Internet, social media, TV, and some video games. They are being bombarded with pressure everywhere. Then to hear that other peers are doing it. To get a reason from school to have sex and safely is not preventing them from experiencing.

Teaching children about sex should not be a part of a curriculum, while not being able to teach about me? My word teaches *abstinence* until marriage. The result of this is healthy children finishing school without worry of having an STD or being a teenage parent. Children would also be knowledgeable and do things in proper order, have discipline, and set boundaries for themselves. But, this will not be taught in school. The reason is that the school system does not want to influence anyone toward the "Christian" religion. They would learn how to love me, Christ, others, and themselves. They could learn integrity and obedience toward their parents. Once again, when good is not taught, it will be replaced with evil. You are seeing the negative results of what you allowed to be taught. When are you going put a stop to it?

Also, parents should be aware of the things your child reads and enters his spirit. Parents are allowing their children to read books that are presented in a child-like image that will introduce them to witchcraft. Once children read these books, they become like addicts, waiting for the next one to be released. They are excited about casting spells on people and about different witches and werewolves. Their minds are very impressionable and naïve. Children are sending letters begging to be in a school to teach them how to become a witch. Most of them do not want to get up to go to regular school and do not like reading the books for class. But they are begging for this type of book. Parents, this is what you allow your children to read.

These books teach skills of witchcraft, sorcery, casting spells, spiritism, interpreting omens, and "calling up the dead." This fits into a category God tells us not even to discuss. *"For all who do these things are an abomination to the Lord..."* (Ephesians 5:10-12, Deuteronomy 18:9-12). Is this good reading material? What will this teach them?

You allow your young children to read this, and it gets into their spirits. They desire these things. They are demonic. Parents are supportive because you purchase these books and read them also. How many times have you encouraged them to read the Bible? How many times have you sat and read the Bible with your children? You do not instill the word of God into them. Who do you expect to teach them about me? Are you giving the world the responsibility to teach your child?

Have you stood up to bring prayer back in the schools? Do you care that your children cannot be taught about Christ in school? Please do not be surprised when hear your child has done something shocking. You should not be surprised by anything bad that happen at schools; remember, you removed Christ and let the Devil in. *Where am I?*

"Train up a child in the way he should go: and when he is old, he will not depart from it" (Proverbs 22:6 KJV).

"Christ" Checks

1. Do you support the removal of prayer from schools?
2. If you answered "No" to question #1, what have you done to reverse the decision?
3. Do you see the negative outcome from the removal of prayer?
4. Do you approve of children learning about sex in schools?
5. Do you support the restrictions of learning about Christ in schools?
6. How would you rank the educational system in your area?
7. What is the statistics of teenage pregnancy and alcohol use in your local school?
8. Do you think it has increased since you were in school?
9. Do you think that schools has gotten better or worse in the last 10 years?
10. What do you think cause it to be better or worse?

Dear God,

I know schools are a place where our children go to learn things that will help equip them for their future. The school system has removed anything that may link them to learning about You (Christ). We—the family, the church, and the community as a whole—have failed our children by not standing up and fighting to keep prayer in school. Lord, you see where it has gone since then. We have lost a lot of our children to drugs, gangs, the prison system, and early death. We allowed them to be exposed to the bad influences, influences that contradict Your word, whether it was at school, through watching music videos, social media, or on TV. They are living according to what they have been taught or have seen. Lord, please forgive us for our disobedience and help us to get our youth back on track. The schools need You to run the Devil out. Lord, we are willing to do whatever it takes to make this happen. We are no longer slothful and unconcerned. We are losing our children and we are ready to take a stand. We need Your help, Lord.

Chapter 5

Where Is "Christ" in Relationships?

Relationships are one of the ways people interact with each other—how another person gets to know you and how you get to know them. There are many types of relationships that are established through interaction with mankind. Christ has given us different types of relationships, like that of a husband and wife, a parent with his or her children, family with friends, and coworkers with coworkers. There is also a relationship with the body of Christ. I am disappointed in what I am seeing with my children. I see much division in the body of Christ. I see families that are being destroyed through divorce. I see how my children cannot establish healthy relationships among each other. The reason for this is because they do not have a good relationship with Christ (Deuteronomy.10:16-19).

I encourage fellowship with each other. Everybody has an obligation to one another. I created you to need each other.

Why do I see so many lonely people in this big world? They feel left out, with no one to embrace them and no one they can trust. Many people walk around broken and hurting on the inside. *Where am I?* Are my children so selfish that they cannot pull away from their own troubles to reach out and help someone else? A relationship simply involves giving a little of yourself to someone for a purpose, season, or a lifetime. A relationship is defined broadly as a state of connectedness between people rather than just an emotional connection by marriage or blood.

Husband/Wife

The only relationship prioritized above marriage should be the one we have with God. When He is the center of a marriage, He will automatically become the center of a family. God brought Adam and Eve together as the first husband and wife. He formed Eve from Adam's rib, which shows us how the couple leaves their father and mother and are joined together forever, inseparably (Genesis 2:24, Matthew 19:5). Marriage, the relationship between a husband and wife, is a relationship that should not end until death. A marriage should be formed on the basis of love. When trying to form this type of relationship, seek me. You need to know if it is my will for you to marry (1 Corinthians 7:32-35).

I will guide you in making the right choice regarding your mate. You have to wait patiently because I have someone who is a perfect fit for you, but if you choose not to seek me for guidance in this matter or wait for me to bring them to you, you risk putting yourself in a bad situation and your lives in disarray. Then you come to me crying and praying for me to clean it up. If you had waited on me in the beginning, your life would be so much happier. I said, *"Do not be anxious about anything, but in everything, by prayer and petition, with thanksgiving, present your requests to God"* (Philippians 4:6).

I desire to see my children happy. My word said, *"It is not good for the man to be alone. I will make a helper suitable for him"* (Genesis 2:18). I will make someone for you; you should not try to make one for yourself. I ordained marriage between a man and woman. This is the only union that I will bless. There is one request that I ask of my children: Do not be yoked together with unbelievers. For what do righteousness and wickedness have in common? Or what fellowship can light have with darkness (2 Corinthians 6:14)?

Being in an unequally yoked marriage is a union that will not last. When things are done out of my will, they usually cause you a lot of unnecessary hurt. There are things that you must do to prepare for this type of commitment. The first thing is to, *"Love the LORD your God with all your heart and with all your soul and with all your strength"* (Deuteronomy 6:5). Study my word and learn your roles in marriage (Ephesians 5:21-33). You must take your wedding vows seriously. Seek counsel from Godly counselors who allow me to rule their lives and are adopting the same principles they are teaching in their marriage. Not everybody will give you Godly advice that will keep your marriages strong. Many people will speak negative words that can bring confusion and strife into your life, so you must be careful of who you seek counseling from. Understand that when you become married there may be trials and tribulations.

Your partners may not be able to fulfill all of your expectations. You are not perfect, and you must allow time for me to mold each of you so that you can overcome your problems. You have to do things that are pleasing to them as long as it does not cause you to *sin*. Always keep me at the head of your marriage, not just when it is convenient. You made vows that said you'd love and cherish each other until death do you part, not until he or she gains too much weight and becomes unattractive to you. Do not look for an excuse to find pleasure outside of your marriage. My children have the highest divorce rate. *Where am I?*

Marriage is a covenant. A covenant is a sacred and binding agreement made in love between persons or between persons and God. You should not want to break it unless adultery is committed or abandonment by an unbelieving spouse (Matthew 5:32, 1 Corinthians 7:15). No matter what view one takes in the issue of divorce, it is important to remember my word: *"I hate divorce, says the Lord God of Israel"* (Malachi 2:16a). My plan is that marriage be a lifetime commitment. *"So they are no longer two, but one. Therefore what God has joined together, let man not separate"* (Matthew 19:6).

Parents and Children

Another form of a relationship is between a parent and his or her children. The definition of a parent is someone who begets, gives birth to or nurtures and raises a child; a father or mother. They guide their children along a path to their future. *"Train up a child in the way he should go: and when he is old, he will not depart from it"* (Proverbs 22:6). Parents should be the spiritual leaders in their homes. Your children should respect your relationship with me. They should see Christ in you. You should guide them spiritually and morally to follow me (Psalms 128:1). This is your responsibility as a parent. They look to you as examples and their future usually is a product of your life. It is your duty as parents to teach your children Godly principles. You should attend church and pray with them. You should instill values in them that they can carry throughout their lives and teach their children as well. Fathers, it is your responsibility to seek me and allow me to make you a good parent, so you can lead your household. Your children will love, obey, and respect you. The man's presence in the family is much needed. Men, I created you to be the head of your household. You are not taking on the responsibility I designated for you within the family structure. *Where am I?*

A woman cannot teach your son how to be a man. Your son needs to see a man's presence in his household to make his life complete. You can teach him how to love me by loving your family. You can show him God in you. Children live by what they see. You as parents cannot simply tell them what is right and what is wrong. You need to be living examples. You need to teach them how to be providers for their future households. Fathers, show your sons that you love them and show affection toward them. Let them know that showing love will not make you any less of a man. It is okay to cry. They will fail sometimes in life, but make sure they know that it is important to get up and to keep trying. Teach them how to pick their friends and how to pick their future wives.

Do not let the world or another person take on the responsibility God gave you as a man. Show your daughter how a man loves and provides for the family. Then, she will know how to choose a mate who will do the same thing. Spend time with her and let her feel safe. Make sure that she knows that as long as *Daddy* is around, everything will be all right. Be available to always talk to her about anything that is going on in her life. That is the way I want my children to feel about our relationship. You know that I am always here for you. *"Be strong and courageous. Do not be afraid or terrified because of them, for the LORD your God goes with you; he will never leave you nor forsake you"* (Deuteronomy 31:6). I place a very high value on family and taking care of and supporting each other. Men should manage their family well and raise children who respect them (1 Timothy 3:4).

Single-Parent Household

There are some relationships that take a lot of work. The home is broken. There is only one parent in the home to rear the children. This type of relationship can be derived from various situations such as divorce or death of one parent. In any case, this is a difficult situation. The children are separated from one parent. The parent that is not in the home becomes a part-time parent to their children and misses the opportunity to really know what's going on in their children's lives. In this situation, the child sometimes feels unloved and lonely. The other parent is working to try to make up for the loss of income. In some cases, the oldest child must take on added responsibility of watching over the younger siblings. This situation is not healthy for children. The children have too much unsupervised time on their hands, which could lead them to making bad choices.

The child is usually angry on the inside because the child cannot enjoy his childhood. Their anger turns to bitterness and hatred. This is when the "devil" sends a drug dealer, gang member or pimp to trick them into being what he desires. This is the reason one-parent households are not my plan for a family. The child was created by two parents and should be reared by two. There are some things that only a mother can teach you. There are some things only a father can teach. Both parents are needed in a child's life. They just do not need the tenderness from mom or just the tough love from dad. They need the balance of both. I know that situations may happen in your life and decisions are made without my approval. This is why you should keep me at the head of your relationships. *"In all thy ways acknowledge him, and he shall direct thy paths"* (Proverbs 3:6).

Blended Family

A blended family is a family composed of a couple and their children from previous marriages or relationship. This type of family structure is becoming the norm. This situation takes a lot of work. Only Christ's lead can help you through. It is really hard on the children. They do not have both parents in the home. They feel like now they have to share one with another family. Children worry about being rejected by the new spouse. This could also cause some jealousy problems with the children and the new spouse. Children oftentimes try to create a problem with the other spouse to see if their parent will take their side, in hopes that their parent may chose to leave. Children always have a hope that their parents will one day get back together, if they can just get rid of the other person. Not every adult is mature enough to handle or love a child that is not his biological child. *Where am I?*

Christ is love. How can you say you that are my child, but you cannot *love*? How can you mistreat a child? Why do you show favoritism toward your natural kids over your step-children? For Christ does not show favoritism (Romans 2:11). I charge you, in the sight of God and Christ Jesus and the elect angels, to keep these instructions without partiality, and to do nothing out of favoritism (1 Timothy 5:21). *"My brothers, as believers in our glorious Lord Jesus Christ, don't show favoritism"* (James 2:1). *"But if you show favoritism, you sin and are convicted by the law as lawbreakers"* (James 2:9). You are making one child seem better than the other one. This causes anger and hate in the stepchild toward your natural child. These are some of the hard situations that may arise. This will cause division in a household. But, you can get through them with prayer. You will have to study my word and allow me to guide you through this. *"I will comfort as a child is comforted by its mother"* (Isaiah 66:13). *"Be humble and gentle. Be patient with each other, making allowances for each other's faults because of your love"* (Ephesians 4:2).

Don't use foul or abusive language. Let everything you say be good and helpful so that your words will be an encouragement to those who hear them. Get rid of all bitterness, rage, anger, harsh words, and slander, as well as all types of malicious behavior, and be kind to each other, tenderhearted, forgiving one another, just as God through Christ has forgiven you (Ephesians 4:29, 31-32). Apply my word into the home and watch how I will make any bad situation good.

Women

Daughters of Zion, I have accountability of you as well. You are designed to be a wife, mother, and a sister in Christ. You have several titles and a different role for each one. There is not one role that I cannot guide you through, if you would allow me. You are so used of taking care of others that you think you can do everything on your own. Sometimes you neglect yourself. This type of behavior often breaks down and weakens your body as you get older. I can fix all your problems, but you wait until situations get really bad before seeking me. You have to study and prepare yourselves for the roles you are playing. If you desire to be a wife, you must study my word to know how a wife should act. Don't be concerned about the outward beauty of fancy hairstyles, expensive jewelry, or beautiful clothes.

You should clothe yourselves instead with the beauty that comes from within, the unfading beauty of a gentle and quiet spirit, which is so precious to God. This is how the holy women of old made themselves beautiful. They trusted God and accepted the authority of their husbands (1 Peter 3:3-5 NLT). Also, seek Godly wisdom from some of the mother's in the church who are well-rooted in the word. Learn the other chores such as cooking, cleaning and caring for children. Do not simply look at your mother and relatives but seek me to help mold yourselves into these roles. Do not think that your marriage has to end like others in your family. You do not have to carry any generational curses into your home. The solution for generational curses is salvation through Jesus Christ. When we become Christians, we are new creations (2 Corinthians 5:17). The cure for a generational curse is faith in Christ and a life consecrated to Him (Romans 12:1-2).

Allow me to heal you from these negative things. I will also break the curse off your children. You are not bound to commit adultery in your marriage because your mom did. You do not have to be abused. I am speaking life into my daughters. Come out of depression and feeling sorry for yourselves because things may not be going the way you think they should. Women of God, do not allow the past defy you of your future. You can be a good wife and mother. *"You can do all things through Christ who strengthens you"* (Philippians. 4:13). Allow me to make you a whole woman, one who is delivered, restored and walking in victory. Be an example that the world can look up to. Be a woman of virtue (Proverbs 31:10-31).

Singles

Singles are unmarried individuals. They do not have to care for a husband or wife so they can spend most of their time fulfilling my will. That should be their number one priority. *"But I would have you without carefulness. He that is unmarried careth for the things that belong to the Lord, how he may please the Lord"* (1 Corinthians 7:32). You have the time to devote to doing my will. Marriage is a gift and being single is a gift. I say this as a concession, not as a command.

I wish everyone were single, just as I am. But God gives to some the gift of marriage and to others the gift of singleness (1 Corinthians 7:6-7 NLT).

I know you desire to be loved. I love you and will never leave nor forsake you. I can teach you how to love through me. Then, you will be able to recognize real love when it comes. The enemy will try to trick you. Do not allow your fleshly desires make you jump into something that can cause you years of pain. You have to stay prayerful. The world knows that men and women in the church are lonely and easy targets. They pretend to be saved for a couple of months by attending church services and joining a ministry.

They do this not to establish a relationship with Christ but to win you over. The world wants someone who has a strong relationship with Christ so he or she will know how to love them. The world is aware of the love that God's children have in them. My children have to be strong, rooted and not move until I say move. *Therefore, my beloved brethren, be ye stedfast, unmoveable, always abounding in the work of the Lord, forasmuch as ye know that your labour is not in vain in the Lord* (1 Corinthians. 15:58).

If you marry someone who is not the one I have for you, time will pass and he or she will become comfortable in the marriage. They eventually walk away from the ministry and stop attending church altogether. Then the devil will show up and turn your life upside down. The devil's mission is to prey on a weak soul and attempt to destroy. The devil uses whom he can to try to keep you from accomplishing the things I purposed for you. Then you cry and get down in your spirit, wondering why this happened to you. Then you say," "I prayed, fasted and studied the word so I could know when it is God." But did you hear from me? Did I not send someone in your path to tell you to wait? Did I not send someone to tell you that he or she was not the mate I had for you?

You did not listen to the voice of warning. Now, you are in a miserable relationship with a mate who is not on your spiritual level. This causes more stress; you have to learn how to continue to grow spiritually and be a good mate. Doing so is going to take a lot of effort on your behalf. The things that I have purposed for you will be put on hold. Your mission is directed to please your mate and put the things of God aside. You are bound spiritually to an unspiritual mate. This is a form of bondage. You're spiritual life will not grow as long as you are tied to someone who is spiritually dead. This is why my single children should be the biggest support in the church.

You should be active in ministry, fasting and praying like no one else. Learn how to be patient and do not be in a rush for anything (Philippians 4:6).

Test the spirit and take your time before marrying someone. Learn of their ways, while they learn you as well. Let him prove his love of Christ. There are wolves in sheep's clothing that are sent to destroy my children. The devil knows that I have great things for you and he tries to stop them. While you are single, you should fall in love with me. Your desire should be to please me in all your ways. But, if you desire a mate and it is my will for you to have one, try to keep yourself in good health and looking up to par at all times. You never know when he or she may arrive.

Always be prepared and do not let anyone block your blessings or waste your time with anyone that is not living a spiritual life. You may think that you can witness to them and pray for them at a distance. Do not play with the devil; he will deceive you and your emotions will have you in a bad situation. I said in my word, *"Seek me first the kingdom of God and all of my righteousness, I will give you the desires of your heart"* (Matthew 6:33).

Women to Women

The relationship between mothers and young women in the church is one that needs to be re-established in the body of Christ. There is some wisdom and knowledge that need to be shared between the mothers of the church and young women. Daughters, allow the mothers of the church to guide you and teach you things that will help you in your walk. The mothers have Godly wisdom and experience from living the life for many years before you. Do not think that they are too old and do not know how to handle things in this day and time. The mothers of the church will always take you to my word to help guide you, which is the correct thing to do. My word can handle any situation in your life. The mothers of the church are pillars that have been around for years.

They are women who seek me in studying the word, fasting and much prayer. Where am I in the relationship with the younger women and the mothers of the church? There is a lack of communication among you. I said in my word that the women of age should teach the young. Teach the young women to be sober, to love their husbands, to love their children, to be discreet, chaste, keepers at home, good, obedient to their own husbands. Such teaching concerning obedience and morality was vitally important to the health of the body of Christ. Why? So the Word of God would not be "blasphemed" or reproached" (Titus 2:3-5). There is a lack of this in the churches of today. The young women think they know it all and do not want to listen to or respect the older women. The unwillingness of young women to listen to the elder women of the church contributes to their lack of wisdom. The young women do things that cause them pain and heartache, and sometimes they do things that will cause them to turn away from me. There is also an issue of respect and trust that separates the women. I want to change this. I want women to stand up and be real women of God. Desire to please me in all your ways and do not limit me to fixing your marriage or saving your unsaved family members.

Allow me to make you a new creature, a woman this world needs: virtuous, holy and whole. Another relationship between women in the church is sister to sister. A sister is someone you can trust with your secrets, who will stand by you no matter what, who always loves and accepts you. There is a lack of this among the sisters in the body of Christ. There is always some confusion and strife. You cannot come together and work for my purpose. You have a job to do. There are women holding in so much pain that needs to be released. You see them every day, but they are not letting go. The reason is that there is not enough good representation of women of God. There is a lack of trust. *Where am I?*

Allow me to change you so you can reach out to them. They need to be healed. My children can teach the world how to build trusting relationship with other women. Women cannot continue to carry these burdens around and allow the devil to keep them burdened with anger and bitterness; it will lead to sickness and infirmities in your bodies. This is not how I want my daughters to live. Sisters, support each other and allow me to come into your lives and teach you how to love each other. Embrace and carry each other's burdens. Also stop backbiting, judging and criticizing each other. If you cannot build each other up, do not tear each other down. Let my love show in all your relationships. I do not care about a person's social status, education level or the type of clothes or shoes he or she wears.

I am not interested in the things that the rest of the world looks for in a person. Sisters should not make each other feel low or uncomfortable because of their appearance. Please stop being jealous of each other's. I created all of you in different sizes, shapes and colors. You are all unique. Love yourself because I love you. You have a mandate from me to love each other as well.

Spiritual Father/Spiritual Sons (Children)

The relationship between spiritual fathers and sons (children) is one of the most powerful. It can be a source of great blessing if done properly by the Spirit of God. However, if done in the flesh, it can be one of the most damaging. This relationship is grounded in scripture as I see he role as very vital (2 Timothy 1:2, Titus 1:4, 1 Corinthians 4:15). The role of a spiritual father is to raise up a son spiritually. A father will nurture and protect a son. The spiritual father will pour out knowledge, understanding, wisdom, counsel, and blessing to the son. A father's primary goal is to make the son successful in knowing the Lord, and fulfilling the call of God on the son's life. Spiritual fathers enjoy spending time with their sons not out of obligation, but because they are truly family.

I (Christ) am the prime example of a spiritual father. Look to me as your example of how to be a spiritual father. I only had those spiritual sons that God ordained. *"And He went up on the mountain and called to Him those He Himself wanted. And they came to Him. ¹⁴ Then He appointed twelve, that they might be with Him and that He might send them out to preach, ¹⁵ and to have power to heal sicknesses and to cast out demons"* (Mark 3:13-15). I did not just pick anyone to be a son. They were sent by God.

I did not take this relationship lightly. I gave my sons direct access to me daily. My job as a spiritual father was to impart into them. For that to happen, I had to spend time with them. To make sure they got all the questions they needed answered. I did not ever want them to sway away because they thought they were on this journey alone. Any father that does not spend time with his son is not a real spiritual father. Many desires to call themselves fathers, but there are very few that actually are fathers.

I cared greatly about the spiritual needs of my sons. I invested time into them so they would be successful. I gave them wisdom, understanding, knowledge, and I taught them about God. I demonstrated to my sons how to do ministry. I trained them, and then I raised them up and empowered them. Then I gave them power and authority to do ministry, and a platform to preach (Luke 9:1-6). True spiritual fathers empower their sons and give them their platform.

I am not seeing that model of a spiritual father. I see sons treated as slaves, manipulated, controlled and not trained properly. The reason for this is because of false spiritual fathers trying to take on the role of a spiritual father. They rarely, if ever, share their platform. If they do, it's always controlled. They may require a "son" to give them a detailed account of the message before they are allowed to preach it. The want-to-be spiritual father may tell the son what to preach, instead of allowing the son to hear from the Lord and preach whatever the Lord desires. When I sent my sons out, I did not tell them what to preach. I simply said, *"And as you go, preach, saying, 'The kingdom of heaven is at hand'"* (Matthew 10:7 NKJV). False spiritual fathers may allow a son to take their platform on a rare occasion, but they will never fully give their sons an inheritance. They do this more out of obligation than of genuine love and wanting their sons to succeed.

A true father believes in his sons, and gets the best out of them. He gets the best out of them because he treats them the best. One of my' main priorities was not building my own ministry, but building others. I (Christ) worked diligently to see the life of God established in others. This could only be done out of a deep and intimate personal relationship. Any father that is unwilling to spend time with his sons like I did, is not a father at all. Fathers who don't put forth the effort to spend time with their sons are nothing more than fakes, who simply desire the title of father like the Pharisees did (Matthew 23:1-12). Jesus clearly warns us in the scripture not to call leaders by the "title" of father, who simply desire to be titled as a form of honor before men.

I released my sons into ministry even though they were not fully mature. Character and Christ-likeness are extremely important, and necessary for healthy ministry. A certain level of maturity must be attained before a son is ready for ministry. However, I (Christ) understood that if one had to be perfect to be in ministry, then no one would be in ministry. I knew that this group of sons would abide in God until they attained to spiritual maturity, and therefore I trusted them with ministry. Controlling leaders can never trust sons with ministry. These fathers will always overlook their own faults and see clearly the faults of their sons. They will justify that their spiritual sons are not ready for ministry. Of course, if these fathers have a son in the natural, that son will be ready for ministry in their eyes (even if he really isn't). This is because false spiritual fathers do things according to the flesh, rather than the Spirit.

I treated my sons as though they were more mature than they really were, and by doing this; It brought them into greater levels of maturity. They matured rapidly because I treated them with respect and trusted them. Controlling or false spiritual fathers do not have the ability to treat their sons as though they are mature. These "fathers" talk down to their sons and make them feel low and insignificant. Sons can never get it right in their eyes. False fathers do not have the capacity to treat their sons with much respect. They do however require the son to honor them and treat them with respect. They don't know how to be a father, because they don't know how to be a son.

I trusted my sons. I gave them all different responsibilities. I trusted them to do it honestly without standing over them and watching their every move. The controlling spiritual father will have a hard time trusting even the most honest spiritual son. This kind of father will need to be there to make sure the son "gets it right."

One of my focuses was to see God's destiny come to pass through my spiritual sons. I believed in and supported my sons, so God's will could be accomplished through them. The controlling false spiritual father will only be concerned about his own vision. He may say he cares about the vision that God wants to accomplish through his sons, but he really does not. This kind of father is only interested in getting sons to serve his vision and ministry. The controlling father does not want to release spiritual sons into their own ministries, because he needs slaves to serve his own ministry. This of course is because his calling and ministry are more important.

I counseled my sons to be leaders and spiritual fathers themselves: "*Now there was also a dispute among them, as to which of them should be considered the greatest. And He said to them, "The kings of the Gentiles exercise lordship over them, and those who exercise authority over them are called 'benefactors.' But not so among you; on the contrary, he who is greatest among you, let him be as the younger, and he who governs as he who serves. For who is greater, he who sits at the table, or he who serves? Is it not he who sits at the table? Yet I am among you as the One who serves*" (Luke 22:24-27 NKJV).

In my view, the greatest leader (or spiritual father) will be servant of all. I came serving my sons. My sons did serve me, but I served them in a far greater capacity than they could ever serve me. I (Christ) gave them everything. I gave them power, authority, knowledge, anointing, a platform, and released them into ministry. Compared to how much I served them, My sons served Me very little. The greatest among them was servant of all, and the greatest among them was clearly Me (Christ). I am the example and I lead by example.

Many false leaders (spiritual fathers) exercise the seat of authority in a "lordship" type position. They may never openly say this, but the air in their congregation is permeated with a sense of "everyone needs to serve the leader…it's all about the leader's vision…sons need to serve their father's vision." The problem with this line of thinking is that it is the opposite of what I taught. I (Christ) said that those leaders who are considered great, are those who serve everyone else. I (Christ) said that the one who governs the church must become the servant. This does not mean that the governor should require everyone to serve him and build his ministry. It means that the governor uses his power and authority to empower people into their God given callings. The leader is to perfect/equip the saints for the work of ministry (Ephesians 4:11-13). The scripture does not say that the leader is to perfect/equip the saints for the building up of and work of his own ministry. The saint may be called to be a part of that leader's ministry or the saint may not. That is not the leader's job to worry about. The leader's job is to obey Christ and the scripture. Serve, perfect, train, empower, and release. True fathers simply want their sons to succeed, and to go further than themselves.

True sons will serve their father, but service should always be based on relationship; not requirement. Required service is burdensome, while service done out of friendship is an easy yoke to bear. I called my sons to be in relationship with me before I expected them to serve Me. Some pastors or leaders will not even consider spending time with someone unless they serve their ministry first. Some leaders will not even allow you to "fit in" at their church until you prove that you are willing to serve. We must ask ourselves, is that how Jesus operates? Is that the love of God? I (Christ) got my sons to serve Me faithfully by establishing relationship with them. Whether it's sons serving fathers or fathers serving sons; relationship must be our foundation. That is kingdom.

The revelation of spiritual fathers and sons can be one of the most powerful understandings in God's kingdom, and it also has the potential to be one of the most damaging. If leaders who are not spiritually mature, and spiritually whole; teach this message, they can damage believers. If these leaders are not willing to truly treat people like spiritual sons, they will severely hurt people. The

Lord has high requirements for His leadership. To whom much is given, much is required. Leaders will be held accountable before the throne of judgment for every believer that they have hurt or damaged. *""Whoever causes one of these little ones who believe in Me to sin, it would be better for him if a millstone were hung around his neck, and he were drowned in the depth of the sea. Woe to the world because of offenses! For offenses must come, but woe to that man by whom the offense comes"* (Matthew 18:6-7 NKJV)!

Ethnicity/Ethnicity

Ethnicity is identified membership in a particular racial, nationality, or cultural group and observance of that group's customs, beliefs and language. There is much division among the world because of the different ethnic groups that exist. We are different in one aspect but are still one in Christ (Romans 12:5). So we, being many, are one body in Christ, and every one member's one of another.) You as a nation have not adopted this concept yet. We are still operating separately and segregating ourselves to what is familiar to us. The biggest day segregation is practiced is Sunday when you are worshipping Christ. *Where am I?*

The first thing one need to understand regarding ethnicity is that there is only one race—the human race. Caucasians, Africans, Asians, Indians, Arabs, Jews, etc., are not different races. Rather, they are different ethnicities of the human race. All human beings have the same physical characteristics (with minor variations, of course). More importantly, all human beings are created in the image and likeness of God (Genesis 1:26-27). God loves the entire world (John 3:16). Jesus laid down His life for everyone in the entire world (1 John2:2). The "entire world" obviously includes all ethnicities of humanity.

The world has not only been separated into each ethnic group, but also into categories based on class and power. There are certain groups that think they have power over others. They have been blessed with better opportunities and wealth. They have used it to gain power and control over less fortunate ethnic group. This type of behavior is the root cause of a terrible behavior that has caused a lot of pain and suffering. This behavior is racism. Racism may be defined as the hatred of one person by another—or the belief that another person is less than human—because of skin color, language, customs and places of birth, or any factor that supposedly reveals the basic nature of that person.

It has influenced wars, slavery, the formation of nations and legal codes. During the past 500-1000 years, racism on the part of Western powers toward non-Westerners has had a far more significant impact on history than any other form of racism. The most notorious example of racism by the West has been slavery, particularly the enslavement of Africans in the New World. This enslavement was accomplished because of the racist belief that Black Africans were less fully human than white Europeans and their descendants. This behavior gave white Europeans power over the black Africans. They took the black Africans into slavery. Slavery is bondage: the state of being under the control of another person. The white Europeans used them to do whatever they needed.

Many slaves' treatment depended on their age, looks, strength and attitude. Think of something that you own. Now think of owning *someone* and whipping him or her over and over. This is how some of the slaves were treated. They were thought of as property and not as humans. *Where was I?* There have also been some other forms of slavery or control.

This affected my daughters—gender discrimination. Millions of women throughout the world live in conditions of abject deprivation of and attacks against their fundamental human rights for no other reason than that they are women. In several countries women and girls are forced into prostitution. Women are discriminated against in the workplace. They never get fair wages. *Where am I?*

Women should have the opportunity to live the abundant life I died for them to have. They should not be subject to mistreatment. This behavior has destroyed the lives of many of my daughters. There are organizations that are trying to fight against these types of actions toward them. Laws have been passed but nothing has changed this behavior. Men, I have not left you in control so that you have such power over the lives of women that you can cause them harm and keep them in bondage. *"There is neither Jew nor Greek, there is neither bond nor free, there is neither male nor female: for ye are all one in Christ Jesus"* (Galatians 3:28). Throughout history and the world there has been some form of discrimination or unfair treatment toward many different ethnicities or cultures for one reason or another. There have been many acts of violence toward them. Because of harsh treatment, many have been cheated out of time in their lives.

Some results caused sickness, short life spans and much pain. These acts have also caused anger and fear in many of my children's lives (2 Timothy 1:7). For God hath not given us the spirit of fear; but of power, and of love, and of a sound mind. The effects of different types of racism or discrimination have caused many heartaches, pain and unforgiveness. For some ethnic groups and genders, survival is a daily struggle. There is a lot of hurt and pain in the victims. This behavior is not of God. I died so that you may have life and more abundantly (John 10:10). How can someone made in my image, just as all of you are, think they can control someone else life? I said, *"For there is no respect of persons with God"* (Romans 2:11). How can one think so highly of himself that he can destroy the life that I gave to my children?

I do not show partiality or favoritism and neither should you (Deuteronomy 10:17; Acts 10:34; Romans 2:11; Ephesians 6:9). *"Are ye not then partial in yourselves, and are become judges of evil thoughts"* (James 2:4)? This describes anyone who shows discrimination as "judges with evil thoughts." Instead, you are to *"love our neighbors as ourselves"* (James 2:8). In the Old Testament, God divided humanity into two racial groups: Jew and Gentile. God's intent was for the Jews to be a kingdom of priests, ministering to the Gentile nations. Instead, for the most part, the Jews became proud of their status and despised the Gentiles. Jesus Christ put an end to this, destroying the dividing wall of hostility (Ephesians 2:14).

All forms of racism, prejudice, and discrimination are affronts to the work of Christ on the cross. I command you to love each other as I love you (John 13:34). If I am impartial and love you without impartiality that means you need to love others with that same high standard. I taught in Matthew 25 that whatever you do to the least of his brothers, you do to me. If you treat a person with contempt, you are mistreating a person created in my image; you are hurting somebody that I love and I died for. Racism, in varying forms and to various degrees, has been a plague on humanity for thousands of years. Brothers and sisters of all ethnicities, this should not be! To victims of racism, prejudice, and discrimination—you need to forgive. Ephesians 4:32 declares, *"Be kind and compassionate to one another, forgiving each other, just as in Christ God forgave you."* To perpetrators of racism, prejudice, and discrimination—you need to repent and *"present yourselves to God as being alive from the dead, and your members as instruments of righteousness to God"* (Romans 6:13). May Galatians 3:28 be completely realized: There is neither Jew nor Greek, slave nor free, male nor female, for you are all one in Christ Jesus.

Relationships among you as a body of Christ are hard. There are different issues among the different ethnicities of humanity. Which have caused some to think they are better than others? My word says: *For I say, through the grace given unto me, to every man that is among you, not to think of himself more highly than he ought to think; but to think soberly, according as God hath dealt to every man the measure of faith* (Romans 12:3). In every type of relationship, I see much strife and confusion among my children. Satan is really happy about this. Such confusion keeps you separated and he can work on your minds individually. You cannot do anything when you are not working in unity and love. My children should be able to establish healthy relationships and live according to my will.

There would be so much harmony in the body of Christ and you could stop allowing strife and confusion to hinder my will from being done. Put all foolishness aside and come together in unity. You are all my children and I am no respecter of persons. What I can do for one, I can do for another. You have to live accordingly. I said in my word, *"I will not withhold anything from them that walk uprightly"* (Psalms 84:11). A relationship is a challenge. You have to learn to accept and love everybody. You were created with different personalities, cultures and attitudes. You come from all parts of the world and have all been through different challenges in life. You have made different choices in life and you were all raised differently. Sometimes this leads you to believe that a person is not compatible with you. You decide not to associate with them because they are too different. You are supposed to be Christ-like. I love and accept everybody. My children are expected to do the same. *Where am I?*

Put me back into your relationships so love can rule and my will can be done. I said in my word, *"Is there any encouragement from belonging to Christ? Any comfort from his love? Any fellowship together in the Spirit? Are our hearts tender and compassionate? Then make God truly happy by agreeing wholeheartedly with each other, loving one another, and working together with one mind and purpose. Don't be selfish; don't try to impress others. Be humble, thinking of others as better than yourselves. Don't look out only for your own interests, but take an interest in others, too. You must have the same attitude that Christ Jesus had"* (Philippians.2:1-5 NLT). Apply my love to all your relationships, and you should have more successful, lasting relationships. *"Charity suffereth long, and is kind; charity envieth not; charity vaunteth not itself, is not puffed up, Doth not behave itself unseemly, seeketh not her own, is not easily provoked, thinketh no evil; Rejoiceth not in iniquity, but rejoiceth in the truth; Beareth all things, believeth all things, hopeth all things, endureth all things. Charity never faileth: but whether there be prophecies, they shall fail; whether there be tongues, they shall cease; whether there be knowledge, it shall vanish away"* (1 Corinthians. 13:4-7).

"Christ" Checks

1. Do you show the love of God in your relationship with your family (Eph.6:1-4)?

2. Have you ended a relationship recently? If so, have you tried to restore it (Matt. 5:32)?
3. How would you describe your relationship with Christ?
4. Do you consider yourself a trustworthy Christian that others can confide their deepest secrets?
5. Do you seek Godly counsel when having problems in your relationship?
6. Do you embrace new opportunities to fellowship with other Christians outside of your church or denomination?
7. Do you work well with others in the body of Christ?
8. How many Christian friends do you have?
9. How many are of different ethnicity or race?

Dear God,

I know that you said that of all the fruits of the Spirit, Love is the most important of them all. I know that I am supposed to be created in your image and should be able to love others. I know I have selfish motives in my relationships. That is why the divorce rate is the highest among your children. Marriage is hardly based off true love. It is based off what one can do for the other. I know I have hurt others and have been the victim of pain. Lord, help me to get back to loving. I do not want to allow past pain to affect my new relationship. Help me to let down my guard and embrace all your children regardless of any hang-ups I may have. If I am going to make it to heaven where all ethnicities will be worshipping you, I must get it together now.

Lord, I know that the reason I have a hard time establishing strong relationships with others is because my relationship with you is not where it should be. Help me to be right with you. I want to please you in all my ways. Forgive me for not obeying your commandments of forgiving and showing compassion for others. I get all caught up in my own selfishness. All that I think about is how the other person hurt me, never thinking of how I always hurt you when I do not keep your commandments. But, this day going forth I surrender my will to your will. I will walk in love with everybody. I will restore my broken fellowship with you, Lord, and restore any relationships that been destroyed. Thanks Lord for loving me during my wrong; that makes it all the easier for me to love others.

Chapter 6

Where Is "Christ" In Christmas?

Isaiah 9:6 "For unto us a child is born, unto us a son is given: and the government shall be upon his shoulder: and his name shall be called Wonderful, Counsellor, The mighty God, The everlasting Father, The Prince of Peace."

Christmas is the annual Christian festival celebrating Christ's birth, held on December 25 in the Western Church.

Christmas is a day that is supposed to be my (Christ) birthday. I have seen so much worldly ways come into celebrating my birth. There is so much about buying expensive gifts, drinking and big dinners. The advertisement is used to please everybody even non-Christians. They use Merry "Xmas." *Where Am I?*

How am I (Christ) left out of my own birthday? How do you think that makes me feel? How would you feel if your name was left out of celebrating your birthday? I (Christ) am being removed from my special day to please people that do not believe in me. The part that hurts the most is that my children goes along with this. They help make this a big worldly flashy event. *Where Am I?*

There are other holidays that are celebrated throughout the year. For instance, *Hanukkah* is the eight-day Jewish celebration known as Hanukkah or Chanukah commemorates the rededication during the second century B.C. of the Second Temple in Jerusalem, where according to legend Jews had risen up against their Greek-Syrian oppressors in the Maccabean Revolt. Hanukkah, which means "dedication" in Hebrew, begins on the 25th of Kislev on the Hebrew calendar and usually falls in November or December. Often called the Festival of Lights, the holiday is celebrated with the lighting of the menorah, traditional foods, games and gifts.

The Jews celebrate their holiday without compromising its values. If you are not a Jew, then you do not celebrate. They are not going to remove traditions or change things to fit non-Jewish people.

Then, there is *Kwanzaa*. Kwanzaa is a seven-day festival that celebrates African and African American culture and history. Kwanzaa takes place from 26th December to 1st January.

The name Kwanzaa comes from the phrase "matunda ya kwanza" which means "first fruits" in the Swahili language (an Eastern African language spoken in countries including Kenya, Uganda, Tanzania, Mozambique and Zimbabwe). Kwanzaa is mostly celebrated in the USA.

During Kwanzaa, a special candle holder called a kinara is used. A kinara hold seven candles, three red ones on the left, three green ones on the right with a black candle in the center. Each night during Kwanzaa a candle is lit. The black, center, candle is lit first and then it alternates between the red and green candles stating with the ones on the outside and moving inwards. This is quite similar to the lighting of the menorah in the Jewish Festival of Lights, Hanukkah.

The seven days and candles in Kwanzaa represent the seven principles of Kwanzaa (Nguzo Saba):

- Umoja (Unity)—Unity of the family, community, nation, and race
- Kujichagulia (Self-determination)—Being responsible for your own conduct and behavior
- Ujima (Collective work and responsibility)—Working to Help each other and in the community
- Ujamaa (Cooperative economics)—Working to build shops and businesses
- Nia (Purpose)—Remembering and restoring African and African American cultures, customs and history

- Kuumba (Creativity)—Using creating and your imagination to make communities better
- Imani (Faith)—Believing in people, families, leaders, teachers and the righteousness of the African American struggle

The Kwanzaa festival was created by Dr. Maulana Karenga in 1966. Dr. Karenga wanted a way bring African Americans together and remember their black culture. Harvest or 'first fruit' festivals are celebrated all over Africa. These were celebrations when people would come together and celebrate and give thanks for the good things in their lives and communities.

From these festivals he created Kwanzaa. They celebrate them traditionally without modifying anything to please non-African Americans. These are just a couple of holidays and traditions that are celebrated by all the ethnicities. They honor them with pride.

The point that I am trying to make by sharing info about other holidays. They are holidays that are not as significant as my birth. I am your savior. I came to die so that you all can live." *For God so loved the world that He gave His only begotten Son, that whoever believes in Him should not perish but have everlasting life"* (John 3:16). When my birthday comes it is a big retail promotion on material things to purchase. It is about decorations of trees and Santa Claus. You found another way to advertise my birthday with a big guy in a red suit. Some of my children have service to worship me before having dinner with their families. I am pleased of that. During this time of the year kindness is shown more than any time of the year. I am also pleased but prefer my Spirit allow the love and kindness to show daily.

The high retail promotion of gift buying causes many of my children to be sad. If they are not financially able to purchase the latest expensive toy for their kids. Some get into extreme debt trying to purchase gifts that they cannot afford. Many of my children get depressed as they are either lonely because of a relationship ending, loss of a love one or job loss. This is a time when the true meaning of my birthday should have my children reaching out and showing love. Worshipping by helping the hurt and broken-hearted through kind deeds.

My children please learn of me and learn of me. So you will know my heart and what is pleasing to me. When you celebrate the life of family or friends, your goal is to do what pleases the person. Since it is about their special day. This is my plea to all of you going forth. Celebrate my birth with showing love, kindness and sharing to others about my birth and resurrection. So they can come to know me. *"That I may know him, and the power of his resurrection, and the fellowship of his sufferings, being made conformable unto his death" (Philippians 3:10).*

"Christ" Checks

1. Do you celebrate Christmas?
2. Do you know the true meaning of Christmas?
3. Do you share the reason for the season with others?

Chapter 7

Where is "Christ?" Summary

You decided to leave me out of your daily lives. Let's look at all of those areas and see what has happened since.

Church—You wonder why people are always sick. Why are they still in bondages? Why is *sin* being taken to another level? Why are leaders failing daily? Why is there a lack of respect for most churches and leaders? *Where am I?*

Saints—You just want to use me on Sundays around other believers. Then you wonder why you are having a hard time at work. You wonder why so much confusion and strife is consistently going on. You wonder why you just can't get that breakthrough you been praying for and why you are not further along in ministry. *Where am I?*

Workplace—Some employers are overworking and underpaying their employees. Thus, some become angry, stressed and ill. Some lose their morale and loyalty and do unlawful things to try to make ends meet. There is a lack of trust among co-workers because of competition for promotions and raises and favoritism from the boss. *Where am I?*

Schools—On June 25, 1962, Supreme Court case Engel vs Vitale decided to take prayer out of the schools. In the place of prayer, you allow violence, drugs, gangs and all types of illicit behavior. The dropout rate is constantly increasing along with teenage pregnancy.

Tragedies like Columbine and Virginia Tech are happening but no laws have stopped these types of incidents. *Where am I?*

Relationships—Why do Christians have the highest divorce rate? Why are there so many broken homes? Why are children disobedient toward their parents? Why can't most women get along? Why is there a lack of trust among each other? Why is there a lack of love for each other? *Where am I?*

"Christ"mas Not Xmas—There are many depressed, in debt and sad people during this time. Due to my day not being celebrated with the true meaning of who I am.

These areas of your lives are too important to leave me out. You cannot control the outcome of your life. I do. Leaving me out of these areas forces you to focus on correcting them on your own. Then, you make matters worse. You cannot do anything without me. You can do all things through Christ who strengthens you (Philippians 4:13).

Chapter 8

Where is "Christ?" Conclusion

I, Christ, would like to see the "Christ" that is supposed to be in Christians. You are proclaiming to be a child of mine but you are not living according to my word. You are placing limitations on how much of your time, money and talent you are willing to dedicate to doing my will. You do not want to take me into your daily life. There is no limit to praying and coming together in unity when a tragedy takes place. Once the shock of the tragedy wears off, you go back into your comfort zones. You live your lives as if you are in control of your own destiny. You are confident that you will see your spouse or children when you return from your day. You do not take the time to pray with them and sometimes you are too busy to even see them before you start your day. My children stop taking time and people for granted because things can change in a few seconds. The future is not promised. There is no second chance to try to get it right; once it is over, it is over.

My children, I am trying to be patient and give you time to get it right. It is so sad to me when I think of the horrific death I died so that you could have life (John 10:10). You choose to live the life I gave you for someone who does not love you. Satan wants to destroy you, torment you and send you to burn in the lake of fire for eternity. Yes, for eternity. There is no end. His pleasures last just for a short while, but the consequences of indulging in them leads to eternal damnation. Do not be deceived by his lies or tricks, my children. You must give an account for every "un-repented sin" that you commit. I am a just God. My word does not come back void. I do what I say I will do. Stop allowing the enemy to use his schemes to keep you in bondage by thinking that it is okay to continue to "*sin*".

You can repent many times. He keeps you in this vicious cycle until he destroys you or until you do not know right from wrong anymore. My children stand up for righteousness, and be holy for I am holy. I have given you power to overcome sin. You choose to still have one foot in the world. This is what I call a *"lukewarm saint"* (Revelation 3:16). I know some of you are thinking to yourself that this does not apply to you because you attend regular worship services, pray for others and have been changed from your old ways. You think that working in ministry and paying tithes really make you better. My question is, do you do these things because you love me and trying to please me in all your ways? Are you doing it for show? Are you doing it to get attention from your pastor or other church members?

When other saints ask you to pray for them, do you pray for them or gossip about their business all over the church? When marriages are under attack do you intercede for them? Do you sit back and hope for a divorce so that you may have his or her spouse? When someone comes to work in a ministry that you have led for many years, do you embrace their new ideas? When new members join the church, do you make them feel welcomed, loved and happy? Or do you come to them with a tithe and offering envelope, a dress code sheet and the regulations of the church? Is your attitude so negative that people do not like to associate with you? These are examples of things that have run my children away from the body of Christ. This is just as bad as sinning. You are causing others to lose their chance to know me. They may leave and never get that chance again. I said in my word, *"The LORD hath appeared of old unto me, saying, Yea, I have loved thee with an everlasting love: therefore with loving kindness have I drawn thee"* (Jeremiah 31:3).

Chapter 9

"Christ" Challenge

I know many of you have read this book instead of recognizing the ways you can change or grow. You are thinking of what somebody else is not doing. This book was not written to be a finger pointer. It is for each one of my children to do a self-evaluation, to search within yourself and find where you fall short in these areas discussed and in your walk in general. I know many of you answered the questions with all the right answers just in case some of your colleagues, a church member or a friend was looking. My children, you are always trying to impress someone, trying to appear to have it all together. What I really want you to do is to go back and answer the questions by reaching deep down within and being real with yourself. I know already. I am waiting on you to admit it so I can help you get it right before it is too late.

I am challenging my children to repent of the mistakes where you have fallen short. Start living like you are my child, free of SIN and anything that is keeping you from living the abundant life that I died for you to have. Your life should be the prime example for this world to see. You should be prosperous in every area of your life. Challenge yourself to step out of your comfort zones. Time is running out. You do not have time to keep procrastinating and worrying about what somebody else is doing or not doing. I see their faults and will deal with them. You are accountable for your own soul.

After reading this book and answering the questions, I hope you are enlightened and understand your strengths and weaknesses. Now, I want you to answer this last question: What do people think about "Christ" from watching your life?

Scripture References

John 14:6 Jesus saith unto him, I am the way, the truth, and the life: no man cometh unto the Father, but by me.

1 John 3:4 Whosoever committeth sin transgresseth also the law: for sin is the transgression of the law.

1 John 2:1 My little children, these things write I unto you, that ye sin not. And if any man sin, we have an advocate with the Father, Jesus Christ the righteous.

Ephesian 5:27 That he might present it to himself a glorious church, not having spot, or wrinkle, or any such thing; but that it should be holy and without blemish.

Romans. 10:17 So then faith *cometh* by hearing, and hearing by the word of God.

Acts 2:38 Then Peter said unto them, Repent, and be baptized every one of you in the name of Jesus Christ for the remission of sins, and ye shall receive the gift of the Holy Ghost.

Romans 8:14 For as many as are led by the Spirit of God, they are the sons of God.

Leviticus 18:22 Thou shalt not lie with mankind, as with womankind: it *is* abomination.

Leviticus 20:13 If a man also lies with mankind, as he lieth with a woman, both of them have committed an abomination: they shall surely be put to death; their blood *shall be* upon them.

Matthew 19:19b Honor thy father and *thy* mother: and, Thou shalt love thy neighbor as thyself.

Ephesians 6:12 For we wrestle not against flesh and blood, but against principalities, against powers, against the rulers of the darkness of this world, against spiritual wickedness in high *places*.

Titus 1:5-9 For this cause left I thee in Crete, that thou shouldest set in order the things that are wanting, and ordain elders in every city, as I had appointed thee: The qualifications of those chosen as ministers [6] If any be blameless, the husband of one wife, having faithful children not accused of riot or unruly. [7] For a bishop must be blameless, as the steward of God; not self-willed, not soon angry, not given to wine, no striker, not given to filthy lucre; [8] But a lover of hospitality, a lover of good men, sober, just, holy, temperate; [9] Holding fast the faithful word as he hath been taught, that he may be able by sound doctrine both to exhort and to convince the gainsayers.

Exodus 34:14 For thou shalt worship no other god: for the LORD, whose name *is* Jealous, *is* a jealous God:

Timothy 3:5-7 Having a form of godliness, but denying the power thereof: from such turn away. [6] For of this sort are they which creep into houses, and lead captive silly women laden with sins, led away with divers lusts, [7] Ever learning, and never able to come to the knowledge of the truth.

John 3:5 Jesus answered, Verily, verily, I say unto thee, Except a man be born of water and *of* the Spirit, he cannot enter into the kingdom of God.

Ephesians. 4:11 And he gave some, apostles; and some, prophets; and some, evangelists; and some, pastors and teachers;

Luke 24:49 And, behold, I send the promise of my Father upon you: but tarry ye in the city of Jerusalem, until ye be endued with power from on high.

Matthew 6:13 And lead us not into temptation, but deliver us from evil: For thine is the kingdom, and the power, and the glory, forever. Amen.

Ephesians 4:5-6 One Lord, one faith, one baptism, [6]One God and Father of all, who *is* above all, and through all, and in you all.

2 Timothy 2:19 Nevertheless the foundation of God standeth sure, having this seal, The Lord knoweth them that are his. And, Let every one that nameth the name of Christ depart from iniquity.

James 1:22 But be ye doers of the word, and not hearers only, deceiving your own selves.

John 3:16 For God so loved the world, that he gave his only begotten Son, that whosoever believeth in him should not perish, but have everlasting life.

1 Peter 3:8 Finally, *be ye* all of one mind, having compassion one of another, love as brethren, *be* pitiful, *be* courteous:

2 Chronicles 19:7 Wherefore now let the fear of the LORD be upon you; take heed and do *it*: for *there is* no iniquity with the LORD our God, nor respect of persons, nor taking of gifts.

Proverbs 6:16-17 These six *things* doth the LORD hate: yea, seven *are* an abomination unto him: [17]A proud look, a lying tongue, and hands that shed innocent blood,

James 5:16 Confess *your* faults one to another, and pray one for another, that ye may be healed. The effectual fervent prayer of a righteous man availeth much.

Matthew 6:19 Lay not up for yourselves treasures upon earth, where moth and rust doth corrupt, and where thieves break through and steal:

Matthew 25:40 And the King shall answer and say unto them, Verily I say unto you, Inasmuch as ye have done *it* unto one of the least of these my brethren, ye have done *it* unto me.

Galatians 6:2 Bear ye one another's burdens, and so fulfill the law of Christ.

Revelation 1:8 I am Alpha and Omega, the beginning and the ending, saith the Lord, which is, and which was, and which is to come, the Almighty.

2 Corinthians 5:17 Therefore if any man *be* in Christ, *he is* a new creature: old things are passed away; behold, all things are become new.

Romans 14:16 Let not then your good be evil spoken of:

2 Corinthians 6:17 Wherefore come out from among them, and be ye separate, saith the Lord, and touch not the unclean *thing*; and I will receive you,

John 4:24 God *is* a Spirit: and they that worship him must worship *him* in spirit and in truth.

Psalms 150:4 Praise him with the timbrel and dance: praise him with stringed instruments and organs.

Psalms 100:1 Make a joyful noise unto the LORD, all ye lands.

Matthew 6:24 No man can serve two masters: for either he will hate the one, and love the other; or else he will hold to the one, and despise the other. Ye cannot serve God and mammon.

Revelation 3:16 So then because thou art lukewarm, and neither cold nor hot, I will spew thee out of my mouth.

Ephesians 4:6 One God and Father of all, who *is* above all, and through all, and in you all

.Hebrews 13:5b Let your conversation *be* without covetousness; *and be* content with such things as ye have: for he hath said, I will never leave thee, nor forsake thee.

Exodus 17:15 And Moses built an altar, and called the name of it Jehovah nissi:

Romans 12:2 And be not conformed to this world: but be ye transformed by the renewing of your mind, that ye may prove what *is* that good, and acceptable, and perfect, will of God.

Mark 9:36-37 And he took a child, and set him in the midst of them: and when he had taken him in his arms, he said unto them, [37]Whosoever shall receive one of such children in my name, receiveth me: and whosoever shall receive me, receiveth not me, but him that sent me.

Psalms 24:1 The earth *is* the LORD'S, and the fulness thereof; the world, and they that dwell therein.

Ephesians 5:10-12 Proving what is acceptable unto the Lord. [11]And have no fellowship with the unfruitful works of darkness, but rather reprove *them.* [12]For it is a shame even to speak of those things which are done of them in secret.

Deuteronomy 18:9-12 When thou art come into the land which the LORD thy God giveth thee, thou shalt not learn to do after the abominations of those nations. [10]There shall not be found among you *any one* that maketh his son or his daughter to pass through the fire, *or* that useth divination, *or* an observer of times, or an enchanter, or a witch, Or a charmer, or a consulter with familiar spirits, or a wizard, or a necromancer. [12]For all that do these things *are* an abomination unto the LORD: and because of these abominations the Lord thy God doth drive them out from before thee.

Proverbs 22:6 Train up a child in the way he should go: and when he is old, he will not depart from it.

Ephesians 6:5-9 Servants, be obedient to them that are *your* masters according to the flesh, with fear and trembling, in singleness of your heart, as unto Christ; [6]Not with eye service, as men pleasers; but as the servants of Christ, doing the will of God from the heart; [7]With good will doing service, as to the Lord, and not to men: [8]Knowing that whatsoever good thing any man doeth, the same shall he receive of the Lord, whether *he be* bond or free. [9]And, ye masters, do the same things unto them, forbearing threatening: knowing that your Master also is in heaven; neither is there respect of persons with him.

Titus 2:9 Exhort servants to be obedient unto their own masters, *and* to please *them* well in all *things*; not answering again;

Exodus 16:23 And he said unto them, This *is that* which the LORD hath said, Tomorrow *is* the rest of the holy sabbath unto the LORD: bake *that* which ye will bake *to day*, and seethe that ye will seethe; and that which remaineth over lay up for you to be kept until the morning.

Matthew 6:33 But seek ye first the kingdom of God, and his righteousness; and all these things shall be added unto you.

Luke 16:19-31 There was a certain rich man, which was clothed in purple and fine linen, and fared sumptuously every day: [20]And there was a certain beggar named Lazarus, which was laid at his gate, full of sores, [21]And desiring to be fed with the crumbs which fell from the rich man's table: moreover the dogs came and licked his sores. [22]And it came to pass, that the beggar died, and was carried by the angels into Abraham's bosom: the rich man also died, and was buried; [23]And in hell he lift up his eyes, being in torments, and seeth Abraham afar off, and Lazarus in his bosom. [24]And he cried and said, Father Abraham, have mercy on me, and send Lazarus, that he may dip the tip of his finger in water, and cool my tongue; for I am tormented in this flame. [25]But Abraham said, Son, remember that thou in thy lifetime received thy good things, and likewise Lazarus evil things: but now he is comforted, and thou art tormented. ²⁶And beside all this, between us and you there is a great gulf fixed: so that they which would pass from hence to you cannot; neither can they pass to us, that *would come* from thence. ²⁷Then he said, I pray thee therefore, father, that thou wouldest send him to my father's house: ²⁸For I have five brethren; that he may testify unto them, lest they also come into this place of torment. ²⁹Abraham saith unto him, They have Moses and the prophets; let them hear them. ³⁰And he said, Nay, father Abraham: but if one went unto them from the dead, they will repent. ³¹And he said unto him, If they hear not Moses and the prophets, neither will they be persuaded, though one rose from the dead.

Matthew 16:26 For what is a man profited, if he shall gain the whole world, and lose his own soul? or what shall a man give in exchange for his soul?

1 Corinthians 2:9 But as it is written, Eye hath not seen, nor ear heard, neither have entered into the heart of man, the things which God hath prepared for them that love him.

John 10:10b The thief cometh not, but for to steal, and to kill, and to destroy: I am come that they might have life, and that they might have *it* more abundantly.

Matthew 16:19b And I will give unto thee the keys of the kingdom of heaven: and whatsoever thou shalt bind on earth shall be bound in heaven: and whatsoever thou shalt loose on earth shall be loosed in heaven.

Matthew 13:23 But he that received seed into the good ground is he that heareth the word, and understandeth *it*; which also beareth fruit, and bringeth forth, some an hundredfold, some sixty, some thirty.

1 Kings 17:4 And it shall be, *that* thou shalt drink of the brook; and I have commanded the ravens to feed thee there.

Deuteronomy 10:16-19 Circumcise therefore the foreskin of your heart, and be no more stiff necked. ¹⁷For the LORD your God *is* God of gods, and Lord of lords, a great God, a mighty, and a terrible, which regardeth not persons, nor taketh reward: [18]He doth execute the judgment of the fatherless and widow, and loveth the stranger, in giving him food and raiment.[19]Love ye therefore the stranger: for ye were strangers in the land of Egypt.

Ephesians 5:28-33 So ought men to love their wives as their own bodies. He that loveth his wife loveth himself. [29]For no man ever yet hated his own flesh; but nourisheth and cherisheth it, even as the Lord the church: [30]For we are members of his body, of his flesh, and of his bones. [31]For this cause shall a man leave his father and mother, and shall be joined unto his wife, and they two shall be one flesh. [32]This is a great mystery: but I speak concerning Christ and the church. [33]Nevertheless let every one of you in particular so love his wife even as himself; and the wife *see* that she reverence *her* husband.

1 Corinthians 7:32-35 But I would have you without careful-ness. He that is unmarried careth for the things that belong to the Lord, how he may please the Lord: [33]But he that is married careth for the things that are of the world, how he may please *his* wife. [34]There is difference *also* between a wife and a virgin. The unmarried woman careth for the things of the Lord, that she may be holy both in body and in spirit: but she that is married careth for the things of the world, how she may please *her* husband. [35]And this I speak for your own profit; not that I may cast a snare upon you, but for that which is comely, and that ye may attend upon the Lord without distraction.

Philippians 4:6 Be careful for nothing; but in everything by prayer and supplication with thanksgiving let your requests be made known unto God.

Genesis 2:18 And the LORD God said, *It is* not good that the man should be alone; I will make him an help meet for him.

2 Corinthians 6:14 Be ye not unequally yoked together with unbelievers: for what fellowship hath righteousness
with unrighteousness? and what communion hath light with darkness?

Deuteronomy 6:5 And thou shalt love the LORD thy God with all thine heart, and with all thy soul, and with all thy might.

Matthew 5:32 But I say unto you, That whosoever shall put away his wife, saving for the cause of fornication, causeth her to commit adultery: and whosoever shall marry her that is divorced committeth adultery.

Ephesians 5:21-33 Submitting yourselves one to another in the fear of God. [22]Wives, submit yourselves unto your own husbands, as unto the Lord. [23]For the husband is the head of the wife, even as Christ is the head of the church: and He is the Savior of the body. [24]Therefore as the church is subject unto Christ, so *let* the wives *be* to their own husbands in everything. [25]Husbands, love your wives, even as Christ also loved the church, and gave himself for it; [26]that he might sanctify and cleanse it with the washing of water by the word, [27]that he might present it to himself a glorious church, not having spot, or wrinkle, or any such thing; but that it should be holy and without blemish. [28]So ought men to love their wives as their own bodies. He that loveth his wife loveth himself. [29]For no man ever yet hated his own flesh; but nourisheth and cherisheth it, even as the Lord the church: [30]For we are members of his body, of his flesh, and of his bones. [31]For this cause shall a man leave his father and mother, and shall be joined unto his wife, and they two shall be one flesh. [32]This is a great mystery: but I speak concerning Christ and the church. [33]Nevertheless let every one of you in particular so love his wife even as himself; and the wife *see* that she reverence *her* husband.

1 Corinthians 7:15 But if the unbelieving depart, let him depart. A brother or a sister is not under bondage in such *cases*: but God hath called us to peace.

Malachi 2:16a For the LORD, the God of Israel, saith that he hateth putting away: for *one* covereth violence with his garment, saith the LORD of hosts: therefore take heed to your spirit, that ye deal not treacherously.

Matthew 19:6 Wherefore they are no more twain, but one flesh. What therefore God hath joined together, let not man put asunder.

Psalms 128:1 Blessed *is* every one that feareth the LORD; that walketh in his ways.

Romans 2:11 For there is no respect of persons with God.

1 Timothy 5:21 I charge *thee* before God, and the Lord Jesus Christ, and the elect angels, that thou observe these things without preferring one before another, doing nothing by partiality.

References

Ninth Special Report to the U.S. Congress on Alcohol and Health from the Secretary of Health and Human Services. Rockville, MD: USDHHS, Public Health Service, Alcohol, Drug Abuse and Mental Health Administration, National Institute on Alcohol Abuse and Alcoholism, Jun 1997.

Kann, L., Warren, C., et al., Youth Risk Behavior Surveillance—United States, 1995. *Morb Mortal Wkly Rep CDC Surveillance Summaries,* 45(4): 1-84, Sep 27, 1996.

Data reported by Jill Schmidtlein, White House Office of National Drug Control Policy, Drug Policy Information Clearinghouse, Feb 13, 1998. The data were extrapolated from *Preliminary Estimates from the 1996 National Household Survey on Drug Abuse,* Rockville, MD: Substance Abuse and Mental Health Services Administration (SAMHSA), 1997.

Youth Risk Behavior Surveillance—United States, 1999. June 09, 2000 / 49(SS05); 1-96 Kann, L., S. Kinchen, B. Williams, J. Ross, R. Lowry, J. Grunbaum, and L. Kolbe., www.cdc.gov/ mmwr/preview/mmwrhtml/ss4905a1.htm accessed June 19, 2001.

Ellickson, P., Tucker, J., and Klein, D. Ten-year prospective study of public health problems associated with early drinking. *Pediatrics* 111(5):949-955, 2003.

Grant, B., and Dawson, D. Age at onset of alcohol use and its association with DSM-IV alcohol abuse and dependence: Results from the National Longitudinal Alcohol Epidemiologic Survey. *Journal of Substance Abuse,* Vol. 9, Jan. 1998. pp. 103-110.

Magnitude of Alcohol-Related Mortality and Morbidity Among U.S. College Students Ages 18-24: Changes from 1998 to 2001; Ralph Hingson, Timothy Heeren, Michael Winter, Henry Wechsler; *Annual Review of Public Health*, April 2005, Vol. 26: pp. 259-279.

Conner, Kevin J., *The Church in the New Testament*, City Bible Publishing: Portland, OR 1982

Goll, Jim, *The Coming Prophetic Revolution*, Chosen Books: Grand Rapids, MI 2001

Evans, Roderick L. (2011-05-28). The Apostle Question: Exploring the Role of Apostles in the New Testament Church (Kindle Locations 805-816). Abundant Truth Publishing. Kindle Edition.

Scheidler, Bill, with Dick Iverson, *Apostles. The Fathering Servant*, City Bible Publishing: Portland, OR 2001

Terrell, Kim, *The Call of a Prophet*, Class at the Forerunner School of Prayer in Kansas City, Fall Trimester 2002 107

Online References

http://www.law.umkc.edu/faculty/projects/ftrials/conlaw/virgin-iavblack.html SUPREME COURT OF THE UNITED STATES VIRGINIA, PETITIONER v. BARRY ELTON BLACK ON WRIT OF CERTIORARI TO THE SUPREME COURT OF VIRGINIA, April 7, 2003

http://www.uoregon.edu/~swest3/definitionofsister.htm

http://www.adl.org/hate-patrol/racism.asp

http://www.spartacus.schoolnet.co.uk/USASwork.htm

[i] *http://xroads.virginia.edu/hyper/wpa/reynold1.html* (December 14, 2000)

[ii] Currie, Stephen, Life of a slave on a southern plantation, Sandiego, California, Lucient books, 2000

[iii] Akers Edward (etal) American Passages, US Harcourt College Publishers, 2000

[iv] Akers Edward (etal) American Passages, US Harcourt College Publishers, 2000

[v] Currie, Stephen, Life of a slave on a southern plantation, Sandiego, California, Lucient books, 2000

http://memory.loc.gov/ammem/awhhtml/awlaw3/slavery.html

http://healing2thenations.net/papers/fivefold.htm

http://www.gospel.org.nz/index.php/articles/ articles-by-rodney/338-recognizing-the-five-fold-ministries

https://thebaseiowa.wordpress.com/2013/02/18/ definition-of-five-fold-offices/

http://www.theologyofbusiness.com/ reasons-why-the-marketplace-is-a-great-place-for-christians/

http://www.7culturalmountains.org/pages.asp?pageid=63698

https://www.generals.org/rpn/the-seven-mountains/
https://www.teenrehabcenter.org/resources/teen-drinking-stats/
http://www.huffingtonpost.com/2012/08/23/annual-survey-finds-17-pe_n_1824966.html
https://www.cdc.gov/std/general/condom_use_among_adolescents.htm
http://bodyecology.com/articles/dangers_birth_control_pill.php
http://www.sonstoglory.com/spiritualfathersons.htm

About the Author

Tomeka has always had a passion to help others in ministry and non-profit volunteerism. She is a positive role model and an exemplary leader in the business and ministry sectors.

Minister Tomeka is prophetic writer, teacher and have led many through healing and deliverance sessions.

Tomeka Mark, BS, MA, is known as The Encourager Coach and founder of Broken Treasure Ministry, Inc. She is a spiritual counselor and life change agent to those who are hurting, broken, and transitioning in life. She coaches faith-based leaders, companies and individuals. She conducts workshops, seminars and speaks at churches, schools, and companies.

Broken Treasure Ministry, Inc. is a safe haven where abused, broken, wounded and hurting people can come and receive love, impartation, restoration and life coaching. Where they will not be judged or mistreated. She offers sound guidance and counseling services to individuals and group clients. Broken Treasure, Inc. offers four phases of coaching to SOAR and GROWTH (Girls Reaching Out Women Teaching How) Programs for women and girls. Broken Treasure hosts a weekly prayer call that heals, restores, and break yokes.

Ms. Mark, a native of Mississippi, holds a Master of Arts in Computer Resources and information from Webster University, Bachelors of Science in Computer Science from Jackson State University. She is an ordained and licensed Elder. She is a certified John Maxwell coach, speaker, teacher and spiritual counselor and obtains several ministry and leadership certificates and training through Life Center.

CPSIA information can be obtained
at www.ICGtesting.com
Printed in the USA
LVHW02s1221070318
568932LV00006B/23/P